FESTIVAL CATEGORIES

		PAGE
1.	Air	4-6
2.	Arts & Crafts	7-11
3.	Car & Boat	12-16
4.	Food	17-19
5.	Flower & Garden	20-22
6.	Night Illuminations	23-24
7.	Islands	25
8.	History & Re-Enactments	26-33
9.	Native American Indians	34-36
10.	Music	37-39
11.	Rodeos	40-41
12.	Seafood	42-43
13.	Shell & Beach	44-46
14.	Wine & Film	47
15.	Unusual Festivals	48-62
16.	Monthly Reference Listing	63-64

CENTENNIAL PARK BRANCH

FESTIVAL LISTINGS

AIR
PAGE
1. FLORIDA INTERNATIONAL AIR SHOW ... 4
2. WINTERFEST AIR SHOW 4
3. SUN 'N FUN E.E.A. FLY-IN 4
4. BRANDON BALLOON CLASSIC 5
5. Z-HILLS BOOGIE SKYDIVING 5
6. SHELL AIR & SEA SHOW 6

ARTS & CRAFTS
1. DOWNTOWN SARASOTA FEST-OF-THE-ARTS 7
2. UNDER THE OAKS 7
3. "MEET ME DOWNTOWN" 7
4. MAYFAIRE-BY-THE-LAKE 8
5. BOCA FEST 8
6. ART FEST BY-THE-SEA 8
7. OLD HYDE PARK VILLAGE ART FEST 9
8. DOWNTOWN DELRAY FESTIVAL OF ARTS 9
9. LAS OLAS ART FAIR 9
10. NAPLES DOWNTOWN FESTIVAL OF THE ARTS 10
11. SIESTA FIESTA 10
12. COCONUT GROVE ARTS FEST 10
13. COCONUT GROVE BANYAN ARTS FEST 11
14. KEY BISCAYNE ART FESTIVAL 11
15. ON THE GREEN 11

CAR & BOAT
1. 12 HOURS OF SEBRING 12
2. FT. MYERS BOAT SHOW 13
3. FORT LAUDERDALE INTERNATIONAL BOAT SHOW 13
4. SUNCOAST OFFSHORE GRAN PRIX 14
5. AMERICA'S MOST WATCHED BOAT PARADE-"WINTERFEST" 14
6. ORANGE CUP REGATTA 16
7. PALM BEACH BOAT SHOW 16

FOOD
PAGE
1. ITALIAN FEST 17
2. TASTE OF THE GROVE 17
3. FLAPJACK FESTIVAL 17
4. SUPER BOWL CHILI COOKOFF 18
5. OKTOBERFEST 18
6. CHILI COOKOFF 18
7. STRAWBERRY FESTIVAL 19
8. ARCADIA WATERMELON FESTIVAL 19
9. CORTEZ SEAFOOD FEST 19

FLOWER & GARDEN
1. BLOOMIN' ARTS FESTIVAL 20
2. GARDEN FESTIVAL 20
3. HATSUME FAIR 20
4. RAMBLE-A-GARDEN-FESTIVAL 19
5. CHRISTMAS AT PINEWOOD "A CITRUS CELEBRATION" 21
6. MUM FESTIVAL 22
7. VICTORIAN GARDEN PARTY-WORLDS LARGEST TOPIARY FESTIVAL 22
8. POINSETTIA FESTIVAL 22

NIGHT ILLUMINATIONS
1. FESTIVAL OF STATES 23
2. EDISON FESTIVAL OF LIGHTS 23
3. JAPANESE BON FESTIVAL 23
4. ILLUMINATED NIGHT PARADE 24
5. HOLIDAY FANTASY OF LIGHTS 24

ISLAND FESTS
1. ISLAND JUBILEE 25
2. HEMINGWAY DAYS 25
3. ANNA MARIA ISLAND WINTERFEST 25

HISTORY & RE-ENACTMENTS
1. HERITAGE FESTIVAL 26
2. DADE MASSACRE RE-ENACTMENT 26
3. MEDIEVAL FAIR 27
4. RENAISSANCE FESTIVAL 27

	PAGE
5. PIONEER FLORIDA DAY	28
6. CIVIL WAR BATTLE RE-ENACTMENT	28
7. ITALIAN RENAISSANCE FESTIVAL AT VISCAYA	29
8. FLORIDA HERITAGE FESTIVAL	30
9. RENAISSANCE FESTIVAL	30
10. BUCKINGHAM HISTORIC DAYS RE-ENACTMENT	31
11. FLORIDA RENAISSANCE FESTIVAL	31

NATIVE AMERICAN INDIANS

1. MICCOSUKEE INDIAN ARTS FESTIVAL 34
2. SEMINOLE ARTS & CRAFTS 36
3. SWAMP CABBAGE FESTIVAL 36
4. SEMINOLE TRIBAL FAIR POW-WOW & PROFESSIONAL RODEO 36

MUSIC

1. SARASOTA JAZZ 37
2. BLUEGRASS FEST 37
3. BLUEGRASS KISSIMMEE 37
4. INTERNATIONAL CARILLON FESTIVAL . 38
5. HOLLYWOOD JAZZ 38
6. RIVERWALK BLUES 38
7. FALL FEST 39
8. FLORIDA STATE CHAMPIONSHIP BLUEGRASS FESTIVAL 39

RODEOS

1. ARCADIA RODEO 40
2. ORANGE BLOSSOM STATE CHAMPIONSHIP PRO RODEO 40
3. WESTFAIR-BIGGEST RODEO IN THE EAST 41
4. FLORIDA "CRACKER" TRAIL RIDE 41

SEAFOOD

1. SEAFOOD FEST 42
2. JOHN'S PASS SEAFOOD FESTIVAL 42
3. RUSKIN SEAFOOD & ARTS
4. GRANT SEAFOOD FESTIVAL 43
5. EVERGLADES SEAFOOD FESTIVAL 43

	PAGE

SHELL & BEACH

1. SHARKS TOOTH & SEAFOOD FEST 44
2. BOYNTON BEACH G.A.L.A. 44
3. SANIBEL SHELL FAIR 46
4. LIGHTHOUSE GALLERY FINE ART FESTIVAL 46
5. SANDSCULPTING FESTIVAL 46

WINE & FILM

1. INTERNATIONAL FILM FESTIVAL 47
2. FLORIDA WINEFEST 47
3. FOOD & WINE APPRECIATION WEEKEND 47

UNUSUAL FESTS

1. GASPARILLA PIRATE FEST 48
2. RIVER DAYZ & SEAFOOD SAMPLER 48
3. GOOMBAY 50
4. SUNSETS AT PIER 60 50
5. POKER RUN 51
6. C.C.C. FESTIVAL 51
7. INTERNATIONAL PAVILION ON-THE-WATERWAY 52
8. INTERNATIONAL ART & ANTIQUE FAIR 52
9. ART & DESIGN FAIR 52
10. INTERNATIONAL FOOD & WINE FAIR 52
11. SUNFEST 53
12. PUMPKIN FESTIVAL 53
13. FELLSMERE FROGLEG FESTIVAL 54
14. MARDI GRAS LAKE WALES 55
15. SAILOR CIRCUS 57
16. PIONEER PARK DAYS 58
17. RATTLESNAKE FESTIVAL 58
18. MELBOURNE HARBOR FESTIVAL 58
19. QUILT & ANTIQUE SHOW 59
20. ART DECO WEEKEND 59
21. FANTASY FEST 60
22. IRISH FEST 61
23. 'HOLIDAY' MAIN STREET 61
24. FLORIDA "STATE" FAIR 62
25. SCOTTISH HIGHLAND GAMES 62

FLORIDA INTERNATIONAL AIR SHOW
Since 1981
MARCH - LAST WEEKEND   ATTEND 50,000

On spacious grounds of old 1941 Army Air Field. Historic aircraft display. Plane Rides. "Bird" vendor booths. Unique experimental aircraft display.

GOLDEN KNIGHTS Precision Parachute Teams---Daring Acrobatic Sky Performers---Gliding Swooping Maneuvers Of Airshow Teams---Blue Angels Or Thunderbirds---Many "Chowdown" Booths.

Punta Gorda Fl   2 Days   941-639-2222

WINTERFEST AIR SHOW
Since 1996
DEC - 1ST SAT   ATTEND 10,000

Event is also a "fly-in", so bring your "bird". All happens at Z-Hills municipal airport, home to Florida's famous skydivers.

Pilots order-of-the-day are zipping, swooping loop-de-loops & wing-strolls---Ground Aircraft Display---Crown Pleaser Are Professional SKYDIVERS---True & Hobby Crafts---Great Viewing, Bring Chairs---Goodies To Gobble.

Zephyrhills Fl   Municipal Airport   1 Day   813-782-1913

SUN 'N FUN E.E.A. FLY-IN
Since 1974
APRIL   NEXT LAST WEEKEND   ATTEND 650,000

A rollicking extravaganza from "landing to leaving". 2,300 showplanes register. 3,600 volunteers make event work. Visitors from 70 nations. 2nd largest fly-in in America! Many WARBIRDS displayed. Permanent MUSEUM.

(Tiny) Experimentals "Buzzing" Aloft---Heavy Attendance At Forums (Main Message Being) "There-R-Bold-Pilots & Old-Pilots . . . . . There-R-No-Old, Bold-Pilots!---Ultra-Lights---Acrobatic Teams---BALLOON RACES---Military Precision Flights.

Lakeland Fl   Linder Airport   5 Days   941-688-8551

BRANDON BALLOON CLASSIC
Since 1981
DEC - 1ST WEEKEND   ATTEND 12,000

Launchings at historic (1870's) grove town of SYDNEY (70 acre) Pass Park. Launches begin 7:15 a.m. Sat & Sun. Pilots vie in Hare & Hound Race. Other highlight is TARGET CONTEST (sandbags dropped on ground target). Parachutists, music, fireworks.

50 Balloons Rise Like A Rainbow Of Easter Eggs---13 To 16 Stories Tall Weighing Over 1,000 Pounds---$10,000 Purse---Don't Miss Sat Sunset "BALLOON GLOW" As 50 Craft Simultaneously Fire-Up Burners To Create A Magical Glowing Effect---Shaped Balloons Include (Snowman, Pumpkin, Sunny-Boy)!!! This Is MY Favorite Festival Because It Makes Me Feel "Child-Like" Once More---Bring Blankets, Lawn Chairs.

Brandon Fl   East On Hwy 60 To Sydney   3 Days   813-689-1221

Z-HILLS BOOGIE SKYDIVING
Since 1972
WEEK PRIOR TO EASTER   ATTEND 2,500

Great spectator event!!! Site is large rural air field with ample green spaces for visitors. Action packed with plane take-offs & touch downs all day. Hard Dock Cafe serving good food & beverage.

Jumps Are From 14,500 ft to 19,500 ft---40 Way (People) Jumps Require Skill & Precision---As Jumpers Free Fall, Touch, Let Go & Reform They Appear As Frolicking Birds---Awesome Dives Are Roomdive With (Loops), 40 Way Penta Arrowhead & 40 Person STAR---2 More Boogies Are 2 Weeks Spanning XMAS And 2 Weeks Spanning Thanksgiving.

Zephyrhills Fl   Z-Hills Airport   800-404-9399   813-783-9399

SHELL AIR & SEA SHOW
Since 1995
MAY - 1ST OR 2ND WEEKEND   ATTEND 3.5 MILLION

America's largest air show. First year's attendance alone was 800,000. Now one of the world's largest spectator events, it is a "Salute to the U.S. Military". The latest military precision aircraft roar down a 4 mile stretch of beach over the ocean. The Pentagon pulls out all the "bells & whistles" for this show. All 5 branches of U.S. Military participate!!! An hour long T.V. "Special" is aired by ESPN nationwide & in foreign countries. Center stage for the show is usually near A-1-A beachfront at Birch State Park . . . . . There are non-stop flyovers from noon till 5 p.m. Visitors are able to meet the "right-stuff" guys & gals at a welcome kick off party in their honor. All the shake, rattle and rollin' isn't in the skies. Saturday night there is a FREE beach concert extravaganza with 50,000 folks keeping the beat and later a dramatic display of light smoke & noise (FIREWORKS).

8,000 Spectator BOATS Attend & Lots Of Rooftop Viewing ---Flyover Demos Include B-2 Stealth Bomber, Marine Corps AV-8B Harrier Jet, Awacs, AirForce Thunderbirds, Navy F-14 Tomcats, B-52 Stratofortress, Army Apache Helicopter, F1 ANG F-16 Fighting Falcon, C-130 Hercules, In-Flight Refueling, Elite Brazilian Air Force Smoke Squadron, And Other "Billion Buck" Aircraft---Parachute Teams dive From 2 Miles Up Trailing Smoke, Moving At 150 MPH and Landing On 5 Foot Target---Civilian Acrobatic Teams---Hang Gliding Demos & Motorized Parachute Flying---Ocean Powerboat Races (Speeds To 100 MPH)---Water Hovercraft Demo Skims 8 Inches Above Surface AT 60 MPH---HUMAN POWER SUBMARINE RACES---At Display Village (Corner A-1-A & Sunrise Bl) See New Speed Boat & Pleasure Craft, Humvee Plus Amphibious Vehicles Also 50 Additional Exhibits---Many Food Courts---This Festival Is A "Humdinger". Bring Ear Plugs!!!

Ft Lauderdale Fl   2 Days   954-527-8766
Beaches Between Oakland Park Bl & 17 St Causeway

DOWNTOWN SARASOTA FEST-OF-THE-ARTS
Since 1987
FEB - 2ND WEEKEND   ATTEND 85,000
A "biggie" sprinkled about the prettiest tropically planted avenues in Florida with streets named Orange, Lemon Lime!!! GALLERY LEVEL works.

Ranked 56th Best In U.S.---225 Artist---Lithographs, Life-Size Bronze ($10,000) Wide Range Of Medium---Bring Money, Unique Pieces Sell Quickly---World Style Food Court---Entertainment Stage

Sarasota Fl   Historic Downtown Main St   2 Days   941-955-8187

UNDER THE OAKS
Since 1951
MARCH - 2ND WEEKEND   ATTEND 50,000
On banks of Indian River with an umbrella of tall oaks. Meander trimmed walks lined with top artist's creations. Park is 54 acres of emerald green.

Juried Show---High-Quality As Just 225 Artists Accepted From 500 Applicants---Food & Live Entertainment---On Grounds Is $2,000,000 (34,000 Sq Ft) CENTER FOR THE ARTS, A Must See

Vero Beach Fl   3001 Riverside Pk Dr   2 Days   561-231-0707

MEET ME DOWNTOWN
Since 1982
MARCH - 1ST WEEKEND   ATTEND 150,000
Really large juried show. Strung along graciously landscaped Mizner Boulevard. Exhibitors from many states & always more on wait list!

400 Artists, Crafters (Best Of Best)---Kid's Rides---Stage Happenings---Classic Buggy Show---Strolling Acts---Don't Go Hungry Food Court---Come, Rub Elbows In An Elegant Setting

Boca Raton Fl   3 Days   561-395-4433
Near Mizner Park On Mizner Bl

MAYFAIRE-BY-THE LAKE
Since 1974
MAY - MOTHER'S DAY WEEKEND   ATTEND 20,000

Outdoor art show circles beautiful Lake Morton, home to 50 gliding S-W-A-N-S (pride of Lakeland). 180 selected artists. Childrens Art Street. Ample & varied food.

Night-light Party At Munn Park---Street Dance---Horse & Carriage Rides---Jewelry---Awards To $21,000---See Prestigious POLK MUSEUM OF ART (37,000 sq ft)

Lakeland Fl   2 Days   941-688-7743

BOCA FEST
Since 1987
JAN - MID WEEKEND   ATTEND 100,000

Extraordinary outside gallery. Magnet for enormous crowds. "Creations" never found in a mall. One of top 200 events in U.S.

Juried Show---Innovative Artist & Discriminating Buyers---SCULPTURES In All Mediums---Fine Jewelry, Oil, Acrylic, Watercolors---300 Recognized Artists From 30 States---Street Performers & Savory Cooking Booths

Boca Raton Fl   2 Days   954-472-3755

ART FEST BY-THE-SEA
Since 1986
MARCH - MID WEEKEND   ATTEND 102,000

Fest closes a mile-long stretch of ocean road, A1A. A mix of culture, art, music, food & fun under "el sol"!! All original work. Show rated 78 of top 10,000 in states.

Bite Into "International" Food Court Booths---Shuttles---250 Talented Exhibitors---I Loved & (Bought) Lucite Sculpture--- A Stroll Beside Oceanwaves, Listening To Instrumental "Combos" And Art For The Heart . . . . YOU CAN'T MISS!!!

Juno Beach (Jupiter) Fl   2 Days   561-746-7111

OLD HYDE PARK VILLAGE ART FEST
Since 1989

OCT - 1ST WEEKEND & FEB LATE   ATTEND 45,000

Setting is London, England style shop village. Promenade streets showcase 150 "upscale" artists. Neat quality restaurants & SIDE-WALK BISTROS.

Mixed Media---Good Family Show---Visit Nearby Charming Residential Area Of "New Suburb Beautiful"

| Tampa Fl | Swann & Rome Aves | 2 Days | 813-962-0388 |

DOWNTOWN DELRAY FESTIVAL OF ARTS
Since 1989

JAN - 2ND WEEKEND   ATTEND 50,000

"Purrtiest" location possible. Between yacht-filled Intracoastal Waterway & Atlantic Ocean Hwy A1A! 200 exhibitors, many from cross-country. Several blocks downtown historic renovation.

Dynamite Artistic Talent---Live Music Includes Haunting Strains Of Indian Sitar & Indian Andes. All Types of "Tummy-Tempting" Tents

| Delray Fl | Atlantic Ave | 2 Days | 561-278-0424 |

LAS OLAS ART FAIR
Since 1987

JAN & FEB - 1ST WEEKENDS & SEPT - WEEKEND AFTER LABOR DAY   ATTEND 150,000

Held in scenic area called, THE VENICE OF AMERICA!! 1,500 artists apply. Only 300 accepted. So popular it is held in (3 parts).

Time For Art Patrons To Dialogue With The "Pros" --- Sculpture In Bronze & Stone---Celebrity Painters---Fused Glass, Pottery, Exquisite Jewels & On & On & On---Stirring Music & Always "The Food"

| Ft Lauderdale Fl | Las Olas Bl | 2 Days | 954-462-6000 |

NAPLES DOWNTOWN FESTIVAL OF THE ARTS
Since 1988
MARCH - LATE WEEKEND   ATTEND 75,000
A 5th avenue MARDI GRAS night street party jump starts the fest. Outdoor themed "dance-halls" throng jammed with merry men & maids. A most "jolly" party!!

Held On 6 Tropical Scenic Blocks Of 5th Ave (South)---The New Dali's & Renoir's Are Of National Repute---Fest Ranks 16 Of 10,000---300 Artist Showing All Mediums---Creative Food Courts---Live Bands

Naples Fl   5th Ave South   2 Days   941-262-6376

SIESTA FIESTA
Since 1978
APRIL - 4TH WEEKEND   ATTEND 55,000
Last premier "season" show. Trolley to island from Sarasota. Juried show of 250 artists & 60 artisans. Island "Village Area" anchors show.

Food Court & Local Hot-Spots For Dining---Live Entertainment---Prepare To "Rub-Elbows" As Event Is A Favorite

Siesta Key Fl   Near Sarasota   2 Days   941-349-3800

COCONUT GROVE ARTS FEST
Since 1963
FEB - MIDDLE   ATTEND 700,000
Extravaganza extraordinaire. In Bayfront Park next to Biscayne Bay. 300 artists (13 medium) swath "grove village" lanes. Music is cool jazz, hot salsa, "plus".

Visual Arts (Incomparable)---Culinary Arts (Exotic)---Performing Arts (Vibrant)---DON'T MISS IT!!!!

Coconut Grove Fl   3 Days   305-444-7270

COCONUT GROVE BANYAN ARTS FEST
Since 1976
NOV - 2ND WEEKEND   ATTEND 40,000
Multi-street fair in lovely C.G. Juried fine artists (130) mixed media. Miami Philharmonic perform.
   Horticultural Center With Rare Orchids & Tropical Plants (Display & Sale)---Succulent Food Offerings---Exhibits In The "BARNACLE" (Historic Home)
Coconut Grove Fl   2 Days   305-444-7270

KEY BISCAYNE ART FESTIVAL
Since 1964
JAN - LAST FULL WEEKEND   ATTEND 25,000
Event shoelaces through lush tropical plantings on Crandon Bl & it's spacious green park fronting the beaches. ISLAND is a vivid jewel in Florida's crown.
   160 Exhibitors---Local "Chowder Chompers Marching Patriotic Band" Is Crowd Pleaser!---Jewelry, Sculpture, Painting, Mixed Media, Photography, Crafts---Wandering Musicians, Extensive Cuisine---Sat. Night Show Stopper
Village Of Key Biscayne Fl   2 Days   305-361-5207

ON THE GREEN
Since 1970
JAN - 2ND WEEKEND   ATTEND 15,000
Site is spacious park in business area. Playground & sport complex on grounds.
   Acrylics Pastels Photography Sculpture Original Crafts---Plus (4) more categories---Judging Awards & Best Of Show---Food & Music Areas
Ft Pierce Fl   2 Days   561-595-9999
Lawnwood Park Virginia Ave

12 HOURS OF SEBRING
Since 1952
MARCH - 2ND OR 3RD WEEKEND   EST ATTEND 96,000

Been there, done that. (Twice) Its' an International Grand Prix Event equal to the 24 Hours of Le Mans. Noisy & exciting 17-turn circuit raceway.... Zippy race cars left me awestruck but so did the G-A-R-B of "race fans".... Holy Cow!!! Bring LAWN CHAIRS (you're not trapped in grandstand seats).

3 Day Event • 3.7 Mile Track • Trackside Parking & Camping • 400 Acres • Best Views - Pit Boxes & Hairpin Curve • 1,400 Rooms Within 20 Miles • View Mounds, Picnic Tables, Playground

Sebring Fl   **1 Day**   **800-626-7223**   **941-655-1442**

TRACK FOCUS:
Sebring International Raceway
12-Hour Race Records

Fastest Qualifying Speed: 133 mph in 1986---Porsche
Largest Margin Of Victory: 12 laps in 1967
Fastest Race Lap: 130 mph in 1986---Porsche
Largest Start Field: 84 Cars in 1983
Most Caution Time: 5 hours 55 min. in 1993
Most Sebring Starts: 24 By Hurley Haywood

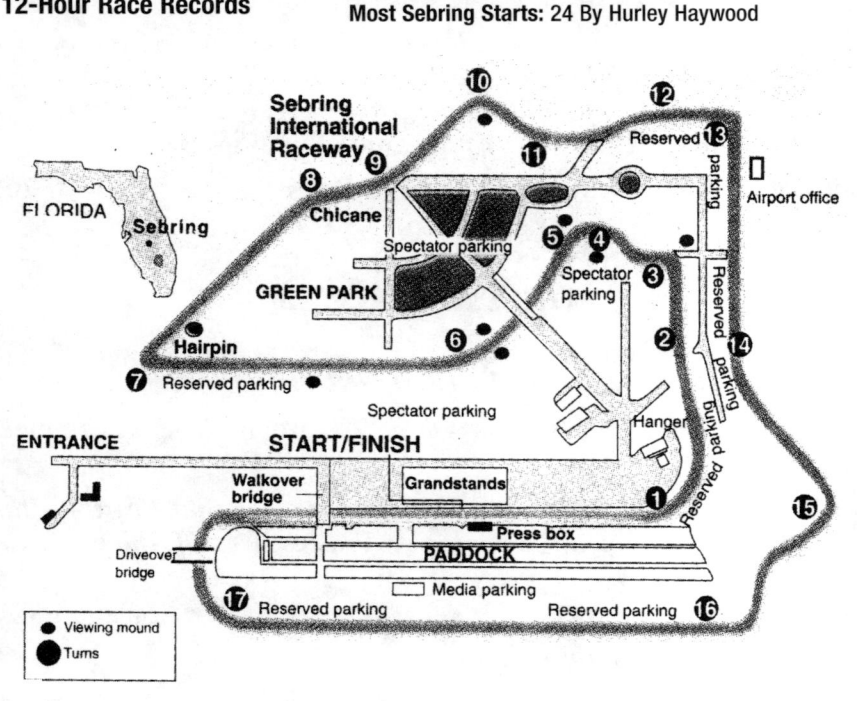

FT MYERS BOAT SHOW
Since 1972

NOV - 2ND WEEK THUR THRU SUN   ATTEND 7,000

An in-the-water & land show. Near lovely harborside CENTENNIAL PARK. Big boy yachts ($1,000,000) tie up at historic City Yacht Basin. Other power-craft line streets canopied with royal palms.

Over 800 Displayed---Cruisers, Racers, Fishing, Sailboats & Luxury Craft---Indoor Display Also---The 2 Happiest Days In A Boat Owner's Life (The Day He Buys It & The Day He Sells It) I've Owned 4 & Still I SHOP! New Is Demo-Dock

Ft Myers Fl   4 Days   941-332-6120
Harborside Convention Complex Downtown

FORT LAUDERDALE INTERNATIONAL BOAT SHOW
Since 1959

OCT - LAST & NOV - 1ST WEEK   ATTEND A GAZILLION

Chariots of the Gods. 1,500 gleaming "water-babies" itching to be throttled-up. World's biggest boat show spans (5) locations: Bahia Mar Yacht Cntr, Convention Cntr, Pier 66 Hotel-Marina, Marriott Port Side Marina, Hall of Fame. IN-WATER & OUT-WATER Sites. 23 countries exhibit in show.

Show Superstars are MEGAYACHTS (Some To 165 Ft). 100 Of Them Tapeout To 100 Feet Each!!!---250,000 Sq Ft Of Tent Space (5 Football Fields) Flow With Snazzy Craft & Gotta' Have Nautical "Stuff"---SHUTTLE BUSES Drive 2,000 Miles During 5 Day Show---In Water Sites Number (4)---Take Water Taxi (All Day Pass, Cheap)---See "Boy Toys", All SAIL Megas (90-150 Ft)---Documentaries, Kid's Fish Clinic---Stages For Fashion Wear & Live Music & Big Orchestras---2 Day Pass Is A Bargain For A Billion-Buck World Class Show

Ft Lauderdale Fl   5 Sites Listed Above   5 Days   954-765-4466

SUNCOAST OFFSHORE GRAND PRIX
Since 1984
JULY - 1ST WEEKEND   ATTEND 150,000
Speeds of 120 MPH. Bay waves to 6 ft on race day. 60 ft sleek racers. World's largest OFFSHORE PARTY. Land boat parade. Party in Wet-Pits (Hyatt, Quay Basin). Street Party (St Armand's Circle).

5 Day Event---120 Mile Course---Great Viewing (Parks, Bridges, Causeways)---Proceeds to Sarasota Handicapped--- "Run What Ya Brung" Race---Lots Outdoor Entertainment--- FINE FAMILY FEST

Sarasota Fl   See Map Pg 15   3 Days   941-955-8187

AMERICA'S MOST WATCHED BOAT PARADE "WINTERFEST"
Since 1971
DEC - 2ND SAT NIGHT   ATTEND 800,000
Glittering, sparkling yachts gilded like Lady Astor's Pet Horse. A 10 (mile) float from Pt Everglades in Lauderdale to Lake Santa Barbara, Pompano Beach. Intracoastal Waterway lined with almost 1 million folks. Bobbing neon parade takes 1 hr 45 mins to pass!!! Grandstand seating at Las Olas Bl. Less expense is viewing from 110 acre Hugh Taylor Birch State Park (food & drink) sold. Corporate mega-yachts are stunningly decorated.

Thousands Of Homeowners Vie In A Shoreline Decorating Event---Waterway Restaurants & Hotels Offer Marvy Viewing & PARADE PACKAGES (Hotline) 800-538-3616---Public & Private Galas Around Town---"Winterfest" Parade Is A SPECTACULAR With No Equal!!!

Ft Lauderdale Fl   1 Night   954-767-0686
Port Everglades

Grand Prix Race Map

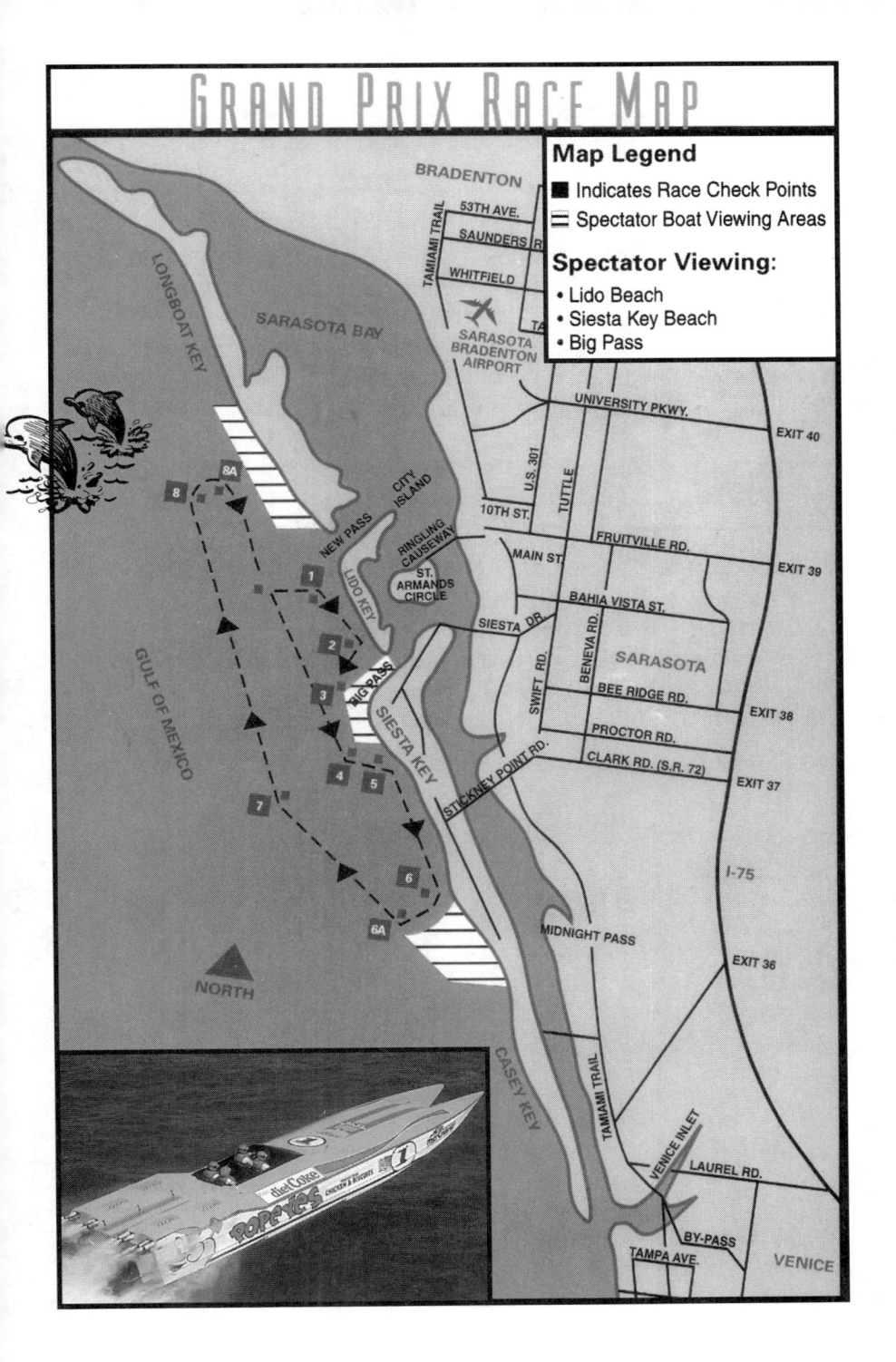

Map Legend
- Indicates Race Check Points
- Spectator Boat Viewing Areas

Spectator Viewing:
- Lido Beach
- Siesta Key Beach
- Big Pass

ORANGE CUP REGATTA
Since 1936
MAR - LAST WEEKEND OR APRIL - 1ST WEEKEND ATTEND 15,000

Its' all about shattering records. In 1997 "the girls" helped do that! (3) of the feminine species powered to 1st place in 3 races . . . . a first in history of 62 year old event!!! Race course circles pretty Lake Hollingsworth. Overlooking the lake is largest concentration of structures (7) designed by famed architect FRANK LLOYD WRIGHT. They are part of Florida Southern College campus. Lake is 3 miles around with fine viewing. Engine RPM's go to 13,000 (your car-only 4,000)! Depending on class speeds vary from (49 mph to 101 mph). Fuel is METHANOL.

> Race Craft Measure UNDER 12 Feet---Weigh Less Than 500 Pounds (Boat, Motor & Driver)---125 Race Boat Entrees---Course Is 1 & 2/3 Miles With 5 Mile Races---Boats Capable Of 130 MPH---Race Event Is TV Filmed Sport Special---American, Canadian & Even Husband-Wife Race Teams!!! I'd Love To Know Their Secret (Never Met A Couple) Yet To Drive AMICABLY 1/2 Block Much Less "Win Races"!!!

Lakeland Fl   **Lk Hollingsworth**   **2 Days**   **941-688-8551**

PALM BEACH BOAT SHOW
Since 1985
MAR - WEEKEND PRIOR LAST   ATTEND 55,000

Elegant setting on Intracoastal Waterway flaunts all Palm Beach superlatives! Under palms on Flagler Drive ($$$$$$$) is land part of show (350,000 sq ft). With pentium chip speed and a car license you may obtain in (30 MINUTES) boat loans up to $50,000 . . . . must be for J.P. Gotrocks crowd!!!

> FLOATING COCKTAIL BARGE Is Great For Boat & People Watching---Over 700 Craft From Back-Water Kayaks To Ocean-Going "Mega's"---My Favorites Include: 81 Ft Cheoy Lee 21 Ft (Wide) & 5 Staterooms, 80 Ft Lazzara With Price Tag Of $3.4 Million & The Queenship 56 Pilothouse (8 Ft Vaulted Ceiling) & "Garage" To Stow Jet Skis---BIMINI BAY CAFE---Gidgit & Gadget Tents

West Palm Beach Fl   **Flagler Dr**   **4 Days**   **561-833-3711**

ITALIAN FEST
Since 1992
APRIL - 1ST WEEKEND ATTEND 30,000
Italians raised cooking from a chore to an "ART". Feast is a lavish buffet of known & new recipes. A (noon-&-night) event.

Pretty Spot Beside Intracoastal Waterway In Green Currie Park---Mushroom Parmigiana, Baked Eggplant, Rich Antipasto, Chicken Marsala (My Weakness) SKY-HIGH CHEESECAKE & "Sinful" Pastry Plus Dishes You'd Not Imagine---Handcrafted Arts & Crafts---Buon Appetito!!

West Palm Beach Fl   3 Days   561-833-3711
Flagler Dr-Currie Park

TASTE OF THE GROVE
Since 1981
JAN - MIDDLE ATTEND 100,000
Self taught course in "Grazing-101". Healthy samples for small fees are perfect. Savor morsels of ethnic & international cuisine from the Grove's famed dining spots.

Chefs Demos---Outdoor Market, Gourmet Products---Bakery---Beverages & Music---Come Starved!

Coconut Grove Fl   Peacock Park   2 Days   305-444-7270

FLAPJACK FESTIVAL
Since 1977
NOV - EARLY WEEKEND ATTEND 5,000
Seems only right that a town called LAND O' LAKES should cook-up a flapjack "fest"! Pancakes supreme dripping in syrups, butter & down home recipies. Entertainment is also a "mix" (midway concessions, art-n-crafts).

FREE Flapjacks Sat Before 10---Parade---Classic, Antique, Street Rods, Muscle Cars-n-Truck Display---

Land O' Lakes Fl   3 Days   813-996-5522

SUPER BOWL CHILI COOKOFF
Since 1994
JAN - 3RD SAT   ATTEND 5,000
Breezes from Lake Tohopekaliga will cool off your palate. Roomy site on Kissimmee Lakefront Park. Chefs take event seriously as it is a SANCTIONED INTERNATIONAL CHILI SOCIETY COOKOFF with winners "firing-up" at World Cookoff in Reno Nevada.

Chili Samples---Texas, Mexican, American & Seafood Chili's---All Have Distinctive Tangy Flavor---Lots Cool Beverages---Country Music & Dance Contests---Arts & Crafts---FACT: There Are (90) Kinds Of Chili Powder

Kissimmee Fl   Lakefront Park   1 Day   407-847-3174

OKTOBERFEST
Since 1985
LATE OCT   ATTEND 25,000
Lots of sippin' n slurppin' in a pretty outdoor Bavarian Beer Garden. Stirring oompah's of ethnic bands. Unique mountain village attire.

Import German Beer, Wine, Soda---Under Big Top Music---Steamy Platters Sausage, Bratwurst, Schnitzel, Dumplings, Dinners, Rich Pastry & Pies---CRAFT TENTS

Cape Coral Fl   2 Weekends   941-283-1400

CHILI COOKOFF
Since 1985
FEB - 2ND SUN   ATTEND 20,000
Lush landscaping of C.B. Smith Park lends double enjoyment. If you tank up on the fiery red dish, you can shed the extra pounds on park's canoe trails, bike & skate paths or horseshoe pitch.

70 Chili Teams---Some Cooks Secretive, Others Share Recipes---Sauce Range From Mild To "Dragon's-Fire"---Multiple Restaurant Chili Vendor Booths---Country Western Flavor Includes Music (Groups Like Alabama)

Pembroke Fl   1 Day   954-437-2650

STRAWBERRY FESTIVAL
Since 1935

MARCH - 1ST OR 2ND WEEK   EST ATTEND 800,000

I used to envy my cousins who got out of school a month in winter to pick strawberries . . . . I didn't know they had to make up the time at STRAWBERRY SCHOOL in summer!! I've eaten my way through this agricultural fest 4 times. It is one of 30 top events in U.S.A. Fat red berries top off shakes, sundae's, ice cream & cobblers---my weakness?? "Triples" on strawberry shortcake!

Midway---Thrill Rides---Smorgasbord of Food Tents---Livestock & Horticultural Exhibits---Daredevil Acts---Headliner Entertainment---Week-Long-Fest

Plant City Fl   7 Days   813-752-9194

ARCADIA WATERMELON FESTIVAL
Since 1985

LAST WEEKEND - MAY   ATTEND 15,000

Location is special beside Peace River and in grass field under canopy of shade trees! Big-time fun to see "WET WILD WACKY WATERMELON WIVER WAFT WACE. Watermelon skydiver too.

Creative Food Booths Serve "Cold Red Behemoths"---Carnival (12 Rides)---Cloggers---Seed Spittin' Contest---Crafts---All Day Entertainment---Yummy Food Vendors

Arcadia Fl   3 Days   C.C. 941-494-4033

CORTEZ SEAFOOD FEST
Since 1981

DEC - 1ST WEEKEND   ATTEND 40,000

Town heritage is one of folks who made their livelihood from the sea. Town perches on the edge of a peninsula peeking out into Anna Maria Sound. Lots of seafare still caught in local waters.

If It Swims They Serve It---Spread Over 4 Blocks---Nautical Themed Arts & Crafts---Local Professional Fish Houses Sponsor Event---Music & Lots Vendors

Cortez Fl   Near Bradenton Rd 684   2 Days   941-748-3411

BLOOMIN' ARTS FESTIVAL
Since 1971
MID-APRIL WEEKEND   ATTEND 40,000
Premier Flowers & Arts Show. Expert QUILT exhibits. Celebrated artist's work. "Bloomin' Block Party (Music, Entertainment). Pre 1974 Auto Show. Horse drawn Carriage-Tram Rides.

Held In Historic 6 Block Downtown Area--1908 Polk County Courthouse---Tour Historic Homes District (North & South Off Main St) Especially WONDER HOUSE AT 1075 Mann Rd---Many Food Booths, Most Popular Is "Bloomin' Onion Booth"

Bartow Fl   2 Days   941-533-7125

GARDEN FESTIVAL
Since 1987
NOV - SAT, SUN BEFORE THANKSGIVING   ATTEND 6,000
Superb array of tropical plants. Gingers, orchids, bonsai, herbs, violets, bromeliads, native & flowering. FOOD, CRAFT BOOTHS.

Nurseries, Landscapers Exhibit---Much FOR SALE---Educational Demos---Stroll Permanent Bonsai Display, Japanese Garden, Herb Garden, Palm Walk & Ginger Beds

Ft Pierce Fl Heathcote Botanical Gardens 2 Days 561-464-4672

HATSUME FAIR
Since 1977
FEB - NEXT LAST WEEKEND   ATTEND 15,000
Hatsume means "first bud of Spring". Bonsai mini-trees. Ikebana flower arranging & orchid culture demos. Underwater realm showcases KOI (tubby varicolor fish) 100's glide in garden ponds.

200 Acres Traditional Japanese Gardens Footbridge & MUSEUM---Asian, American Food, Beer Garden---Martial Arts Masters---Kami-shibai (Story telling) Origami (Paper Folding) ---3 Stages Continuous Entertainment---Yes, PLANT SALES

Delray Beach Fl   4000 Morikami Pk Rd   2 Days   561-495-0233

RAMBLE-A-GARDEN-FESTIVAL
Since 1940

DEC - 1ST WEEKEND   ATTEND 15,000

Scores of exhibits & SALES. Antique & Collectibles booths. Books, Garden Marketplace. Kid area (face paint, hat making, carnivorous plants). Demos (grafting, bonsai, cooking). See Palm Garden (300 kinds). One seed weighs (35 pounds)!!!

> *83 Acres, 11 Lakes---Largest Tropical Garden In U.S.A.---Conservatory (16,000 sq ft)---Sunken Garden, Arboretum & Rain Forest---Narrated TRAM TOURS---Lunch In "Rainforest Cafe"!!!*

Miami Fl   2 Days   305-667-1651
Fairchild Tropical Garden 10901 Old Cutler Rd

CHRISTMAS AT PINEWOOD
"A CITRUS CELEBRATION"
Since 1995

DEC - 2ND WEEK THROUGH 31ST   ATTEND 5,000

Mediterranean Revival Home & Gardens. Elegance (Inside & Out). Stunning CITRUS DECOR.

Lake Wales Fl   Bok Tower   20 Days   941-676-1408

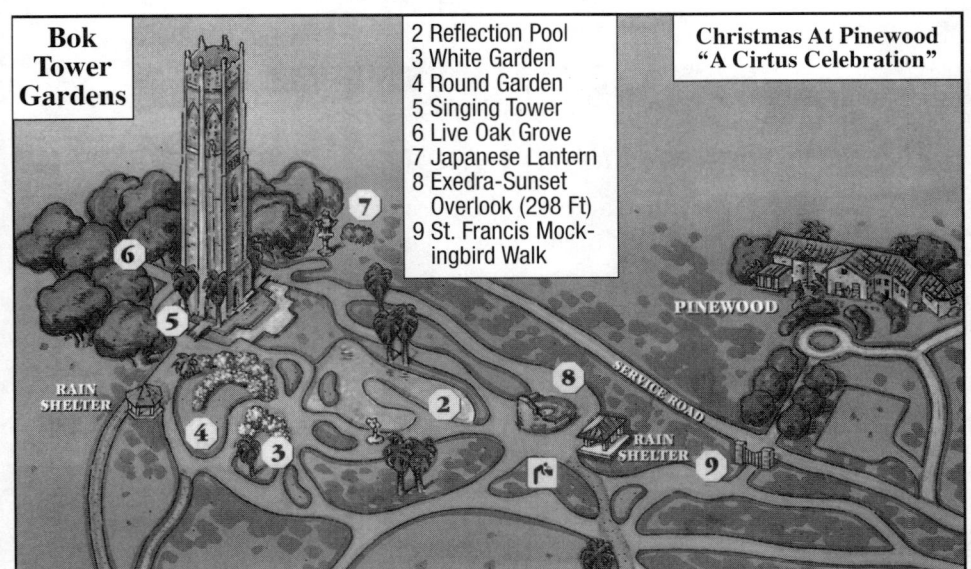

Bok Tower Gardens

2 Reflection Pool
3 White Garden
4 Round Garden
5 Singing Tower
6 Live Oak Grove
7 Japanese Lantern
8 Exedra-Sunset Overlook (298 Ft)
9 St. Francis Mockingbird Walk

Christmas At Pinewood "A Cirtus Celebration"

MUM FESTIVAL
Since 1985

NOV - WHOLE MONTH   ATTEND 2-GAZILLION

No "dumb-mums" allowed. All plants pass TESTS & are certified.

A 35 Ft Waterfall-Flow Of Mums Is Centerpiece---3,000,000 Mum Blooms Of Peach, Scarlet, Gold, Ivory, Lavenders Are Eye-Popping---Mum Displays Include 750 Cascades, 32 Poodle Baskets, Bonsai Tree Forms, Animal Topiary Forms (B-I-G), Arches, Gazebos, & 6 Ft Cones

WORLD'S LARGEST TOPIARY FESTIVAL
Since 1985

JUNE - MID THRU LABOR DAY   ATTEND A BUNCH

Seeing is believing as famed horticulturists work their magic to create a TOPIARY 1800's riverside town. Docked on lake is a romantic 30 ft riverboat & working smokestack. Ivy workmen unload boxes of rare tropical plants. TOPIARY ZOO!!!

An 1860's Bandstand & Members---On Garden Lanes Are Life-Size Victorian Ladies & Gents Adorned In The Period---Topiary Children, Pets Run To Spinning Carousel, Mounted With Ivy Ostriches & Camels---Life-Size Topiary Scenes & Figures Number Over (90)---C.G. HOSTS 200 WEDDINGS A YEAR!

POINSETTIA FESTIVAL
Since 1989

NOV - LAST WEEKEND THRU JAN - 2ND WEEKEND

40,000 dazzling plants. Snowcapped poinsettia mountain range. 15 ft Swiss Garden railway music box. Candy cane bird cage, prancing topiary REINDEER.

200 Acres Pulse With 4 Million Lights---110 Ft Tall Christmas Tree (22,000) Lights---Strolling Carolers---Exciting Splendiferous Beginning To YULETIDE!

Cypress Gardens-Winter Haven Fl   Off US 27
                                    800-282-2123   941-324-2111

Mum & Topiary Fests At Cypress Gardens

FESTIVAL OF STATES – NIGHT PARADE
Since 1921
*MARCH - LAST WEEKEND THRU 1ST WEEK APRIL
ATTEND 300,000*

St Petersburg's longest running tradition (over 75 yrs) the event celebrates Springtime. Night parade is popular. It coils about boat basin & pier. Entertainment is a potpourri of dancers clowns, bands & lights. Sky glows with post-parade FIREWORKS!

100 Units---Sidewalk Chalk Art---Daytime Parade Also---Many Events In 7 Day Fest---Carnival, Park Concerts, Bed Races, Arts & Crafts, Antique Autos, Food Fest (Straub Park)

St Petersburg Fl   7 Days   813-821-4069
Downtown Bayshore Dr

EDISON FESTIVAL OF LIGHT NIGHT PARADE
Since 1938
FEB - 3RD WEEKEND   ATTEND 60,000

About 15,000 lawn chairs are tied to anything that can't move on parade route (2 weeks before event)!!! NIGHT PARADE sparkles & sizzling with tens-of-thousands of lights

2 Mile Route---140 Floats & Units---Block Party Plus (39) More Events Week Prior---Famed Stadium Show---Fireworks ---Nope, No One Ever Bothers The Lawn Chairs!!!

Ft Myers Fl   Cleveland Ave   1 Night   941-334-2999

JAPANESE BON FESTIVAL
Since 1977
AUG - 3RD SATURDAY   ATTEND 7,000

Enter a glowing night-time fairyland. One of top 20 events in August. Exciting taiko-drums perform. Traditional Japanese Dances.

Floating Glittery LANTERNS---Booming Fireworks---Japanese Street Fair, Games & Shop Stalls---Sunset Illumination Of Drifting Lanterns On MORIKAMI POND ---Japanese-Yankee Foods Drinks Icy Beer

Delray Beach Fl   1 Night   561-495-0233
Morikami Museum & Japanese Gardens

ILLUMINATED NIGHT PARADE
Since 1946
FEB - LATE   ATTEND 100,000
Was voted as LARGEST & MOST BEAUTIFUL NIGHT PARADE IN THE SOUTH. Route from Florida Aquarium to Ybor City.

Tampa Tradition With Latin Heritage---Krewe Of Knights Of Sant' Yago Throw Necklaces, Doubloons Trinkets & Treasure To Crowds---At Parade's End Party Gears Up In Street & Bistros Of Historic Ybor City.

Tampa Fl   Aquarium To Ybor City   1 Night   813-228-7777

HOLIDAY FANTASY OF LIGHTS
Since 1992
SUN BEFORE THANKSGIVING THRU JAN 3 (NIGHTLY) ATTEND 202,000

Break out kodak & camcorders. Sky over Tradewinds Park (540 acres) radiates colors. Spectacular DRIVE-THROUGH of 60 "pulsing" festive displays.

2.2 Mile Vehicle Tour---Millions Of Twinkling Lights---Larger-Than-Life Illuminated & ANIMATED Creations---A Captivating Magic Wonderland---Most Popular With Tour Bus Groups---Light Tour Is A "U-DRIVE" And Bargain To Boot So Pile 'Em In Your Buggy & Come See The Show

Coconut Creek Fl   42 Nights   954-357-8100
3600 W. Sample Rd

FESTIVAL FACTS

- Each WEEK 11,000,000 People Attend Festivals

- Top Event In U.S. Is St Paul Minnesota Winter Carnival Begun in 1885 (112 Yrs Old). Runs 10 Days & 1,000,000 Attend

- Florida's Biggest Fest Is Shell Air & Sea Show. Ft Lauderdale 3,500,000 Attend

ISLAND JUBILEE
Since 1981
NOV - MIDDLE WEEKEND   ATTEND 10,000

A merry mixed gathering. Site on 48 acres beside green waves of Florida Bay.

Tasty Bites---2 Stages Live Performers---Carnival Rides---Bake & Eat Contests---Craft Vendors---Classic Car Show

Tavernier Key Fl   2 Days   800-822-1088   305-451-1414
Plantation Yacht Harbor

HEMINGWAY DAYS
Since 1981
JULY - LATE (1 WEEK)   ATTEND 30,000

Historic Duval St (downtown). A Caribbean street fair of tropical flair. Back lanes & main street "ooze" with throngs. Literary Competitions.

Tropic Cuisine Bars---Original Art, Crafts---Look A Like Competition---Music Stages---Key West At It's Liveliest---Visit HEMINGWAY HOME & MUSEUM---Races, Regattas, Fish Tournaments---Great SUMMER Event!

Key West Fl   Duval St   7 Days   800-LAST KEY   305-294-2587

ANNA MARIA ISLAND WINTERFEST
Since 1988
DEC - 1ST WEEKEND   ATTEND 40,000

On pretty gulfcoast island. City Hall Park pops at seams with crowds. Start early as bridge lines require a "wee bit" of patience.

Fine Arts, Crafts---Over 100 Exhibitors---Live Music---Extensive Professional Food Court---Wildlife, Historical & Environmental Displays---Artwork Raffle

Anna Maria Island Fl   2 Days   941-778-2099

HERITAGE FESTIVAL
Since 1975
NOV - 2ND WEEK   ATTEND 250,000
SOUTH FLORIDA FAIRGROUNDS only site large enough for event. Admission fee. Giant carnival mid-way. Rides. Family night (Free Admit). Pet zoo & clowns.

Yesteryear Village Is Actual Historic Florida Town With Heritage Costumed Folks----Concert Stage (Big Names)---Continuous Live Music Hall---Expo Hall (Arts Crafts History Education)---International Food Court

West Palm Beach Fl   5 Days   561-642-4260
South Fl Fairground

DADE MASSACRE RE-ENACTMENT
Since 1980
JAN - 1ST WEEKEND   ATTEND 5,000
200 Combatants relive the battle of Dec. 28, 1835 when Major Dade & 100 soldiers were ambushed by 180 Seminole Warriors. It began a 7 year war between U.S. & Seminole nation. Cannon & musket fire boom next to actual battlefield.

Views Are From Sloping Mound---Narrations By Soldier & An Indian---Infantry Maneuvers, Cannon Demos---Seminole Dances, Authentic Military & Indian Encampments

Bushnell Fl   2 Days   352-793-4781
Dade Battlefield Historic Site

State Park—Living History Re-Enactment Sites
▶ *FT FOSTER-TAMPA (All Weekends)   813-987-6771*
▶ *KISSIMMEE COW CAMP–LK KISSIMMEE STATE PARK (All Weekends) 941-696-1112*
▶ *FT CLINCH-FERNANDINA (Daily) 904-261-4212*
▶ *OLUSTEE BATTLEFIELD–Lake City (Sunday Nearest Feb 20) 904-752-2577*
▶ *BATTLE OF NATURAL BRIDGE–Tallahassee (Sunday Nearest March 6) 850-925-6216*

MEDIEVAL FAIR
Since 1975
FEB - LAST WEEK   ATTEND 125,000

"THY" must go!! Armoured joust tournaments. A medieval village of 200 entertainers. 7 stages of madrigals mimes jugglers magicians & jesters. Awesome "royal falcon show".

Human Combat Chess---Showcase Of Medieval Craft Artisans (160)---King's Elephant & Camel Rides---Royal Treasure Hunt---Brass Rubbings---A You-Take-Part ROYAL TEA---Scottish Games---Free Admit To RINGLING MUSEUMS

Sarasota Fl   Ringling Museum   4 Days   941-355-5105

RENAISSANCE FESTIVAL
Since 1995
FEB - (2) WEEKENDS - 2ND & 3RD
ATTEND 15,000 PER WEEKEND

Step back in time 500 years. On Ye Olde Picnic Island in John Prince Park (1,000 acres). Queen's tea & wedding, Romeo & Juliet Auditions. Armored JOUSTING. Fire Eaters, village market shoppes (tasty treats).

Artisan Lane Of Master & Apprentice (All Handcrafted Wares)---Elephant, Pony Rides, Ancient Games---250 Costumed Actors---MULTIPLE STAGES & Theatre---"Press-A-Wench", "Tote-A-Bloke Contests"---Get Thee Hence For Romance, Beauty & Adventure

Lake Worth Fl   John Prince Park 4759 S. Congress Ave
2 Weekends   800-779-4910   Park 561-582-7992

PIONEER FLORIDA DAY
Since 1973
SEPT - LABOR DAY   ATTEND 5,000

On 21 rolling acres near restored downtown Dade City. Enjoy "ole-timey" days & ways wandering through (6) historic structures on grounds FORGOTTEN CRAFTS DEMONSTRATIONS (30 Crafters).

"Cracker Vittles" Wagon-Pony Rides---Country Music Storytelling---COUNTRY STORE---Flywheel Engines Gospel Sing---Fish Dinner Stompin'-n-Kickin'---Stage Performers (All Day)---Food Booths

Dade City Fl   Pioneer Florida Museum   1 Day   352-567-0262

CIVIL WAR BATTLE REENACTMENT
Since 1996
MARCH - MIDDLE WEEKEND   ATTEND 20,000

Live history of Florida's 3rd largest Civil War Battle. Visitors visit Confederate & Union Camps. Mercantile barn (farm supplies). See antique flywheel engines.

Site is 80 Acre Rural Farm---600 Soldiers (Cavalry Infantry Artillery) Battle Before Your Eyes---150 Craft---Pioneer Trader Village---Hay & Pony Rides, Pet Zoo---Colossal EASTER EGG HUNT---Model Aircraft, All Day Stage Entertainment---Strawberry Shortcake, Endless "Vittles"

Sarasota Fl   2 Days   941-322-2168
10 Miles East On Rd 70 North On Rd 675 Hunsader Farms

ITALIAN RENAISSANCE FESTIVAL AT VIZCAYA
Since 1982

MARCH - 3RD WEEKEND   ATTEND 25,000

America's only "authentic" Italian Renaissance Event. It is (1 of 5) top cultural fests in U.S. RENAISSANCE HISTORICAL SOCIETY of Miami makes it all happen!!! Reenactment year is 1500. Setting is opulent 24 room villa, gardens & forest overlooking Biscayne Bay. I was amazed at the color pageantry & costumes of over 250 actors. Living Chess game is performed on a 40 foot marbleized board. Combat & themed presentations are staged. Actors practice 48 weeks a year. Dining & drinking pleasures include spicey Greek fare, German delicacies, exotic Caribbean food, sweet drinks, wine & brews!

5 Stages Of Renaissance Entertainment---Strolling Minstrels & Madrigal Singers---Birds Of Gauntlet & Falconry Shows---Sword Swallowers, Dueling Swordplays, Venetian Court Ball---75 Period Crafters, Demonstrators From Italy & U.S.!!! (Pewter Goblets, Wood Swords, Masks, Banners, Jewelry, Perfumed Oils, Antique Weapons---International Food Court, Fortunes Told--- "COME, LIVE THY FANTASY!!!

Miami Fl   Vizcaya 3251 S. Miami Ave   4 Days   305-250-9133

FLORIDA HERITAGE FESTIVAL
Since 1939
APRIL - MID   EST ATTEND 100,000

Commemorates Hernando de Soto's landing on May 30 1539 at SHAW'S POINT on Manatee River. Officials attend from Bradenton's "sister city", Barcarrota Spain. This many event fest is one of the top 100 festivals in NORTH AMERICA!!

Night Grand Parade, One of Nation's Largest Illuminated (3 Mile Route)---Stadium Entertainment---Zany Plastic Boat Regatta---DeSoto Formal Ball---Manatee River Fest

Bradenton Fl   3 Days   **941-747-7953**

RENAISSANCE FESTIVAL
Since 1979
BEGIN IN MARCH - (6) CONSEC. WEEKENDS
ATTEND 15,000 PER WEEKEND

Fantasy come to life in forested (40) acres like "Nottingham Woods". Cheer for your mounted knight on JOUSTING field (twice daily). Stroll lanes of the realm lined with 125 ARTISAN SHOPPES. PALACE KITCHENS, 8 STAGES & 350 costumed performers!!!

Elephant Pony Rides---Carrasello---Wee People's Realm & Theatre---Archery, Ax Throwing, KNIGHTING CEREMONY (Daily)---Come, Thee Eat Drink & Be Merrie!

Largo Fl   (6) Weekends   **800-779-4910**   **813-586-5423**
400 Central Park Dr   (SEE MAP PAGE 32-33)

BUCKINGHAM HISTORIC DAYS REENACTMENT
Since 1980

MARCH - 2ND WEEKEND   ATTEND 10,000

Buckingham is tiny community just off Orange River. Back in 1870's it was called Twelve Mile Creek. Federal government didn't think name had elegance so postmaster named it Buckingham. Its' "cracker country" and locals can trace roots back-a-spell. Event held at roomy (15) acre community association grounds.

150 Blue & Gray Clad Civil War Reenacters---Authentic Weaponry & Battle---Horse Drawn Ambulance & Supply Wagons---Camp Followers Tents & Cooking---COSTUME BALL In Period Attire---Historic Country Crafts & Exhibits---Parade---Food For The Hungry---Plus Lots More Colonial Going's On

Buckingham Fl   2 Days   941-332-3624
East of Ft Myers Off Rd 80 Buckingham Comm Assoc

FLORIDA RENAISSANCE FESTIVAL
Since 1994

FEB - ALL WEEKENDS   ATTEND 15,000

Held in Topeekeegee Yugnee Park is most appropriate because "topeekeegee yugnee is a Seminole Indian word meaning "gathering place" and T.Y. is a gorgeous park which hosts scores of events annually. This particular festival is produced by LIVING HISTORY, a not-for-profit cultural and educational organization and Broward County Parks.

Park Transformed Into 16th Century Village---Hundreds Of Vividly Costumed Professional Actors Perform---TEN STAGES Throughout Park Artisan Village (Glass Blowing, Wood Toys & Lots More)---Games Of Skill, Archery, Strength---Full Armor Knights In Tournaments---Feast On Foods Fit For Kings & Queens!!!

Ft Lauderdale Fl   Each Weekend   954-985-1980
T.Y. Park Sheridan St. & N. Park Rd

Renaissance Festival Mappe

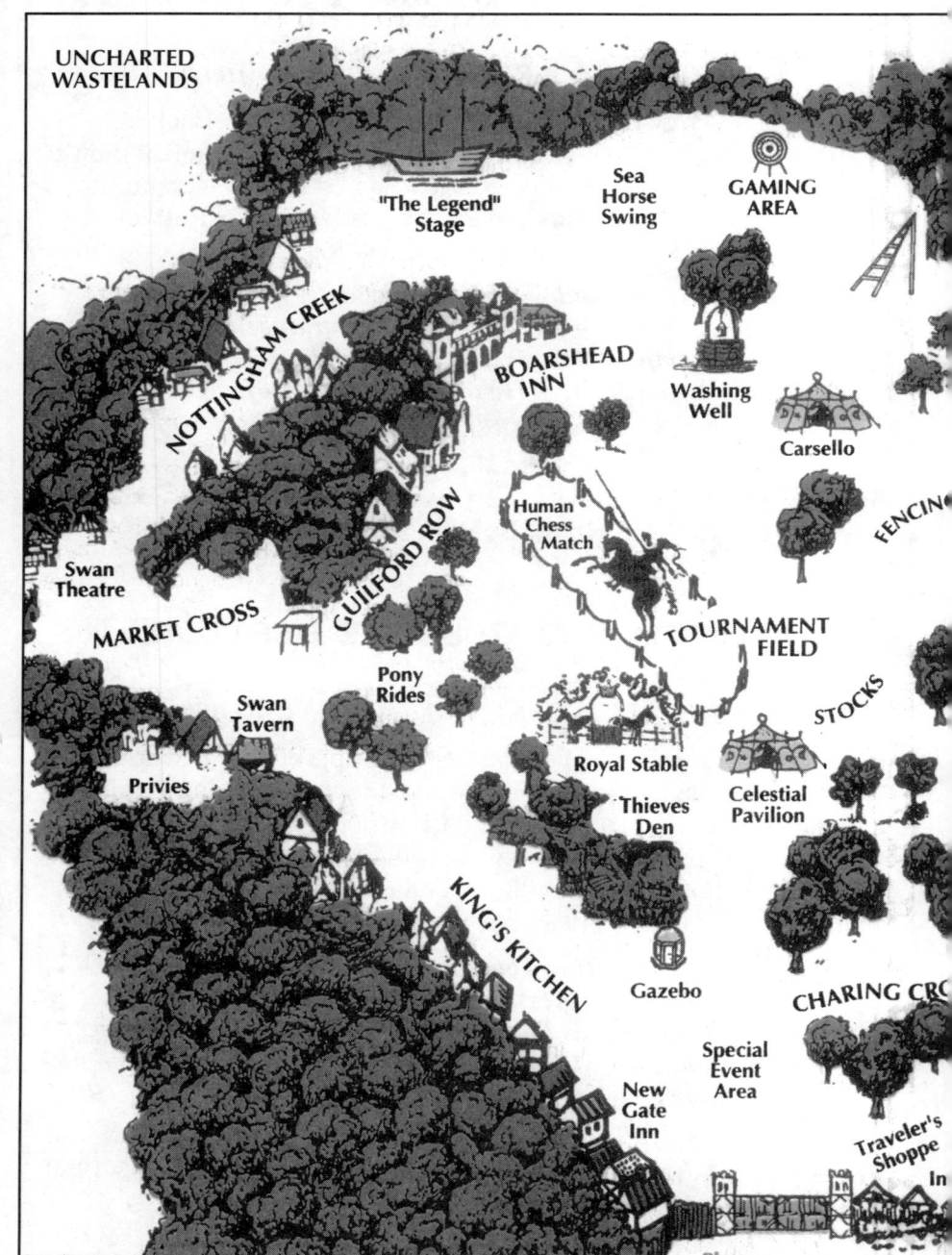

UNCHARTED WASTELANDS

"The Legend" Stage

Sea Horse Swing

GAMING AREA

NOTTINGHAM CREEK

BOARSHEAD INN

Washing Well

Carsello

Swan Theatre

GUILFORD ROW

Human Chess Match

FENCING

MARKET CROSS

Pony Rides

TOURNAMENT FIELD

STOCKS

Swan Tavern

Royal Stable

Celestial Pavilion

Privies

Thieves Den

KING'S KITCHEN

Gazebo

CHARING CROSS

Special Event Area

New Gate Inn

Traveler's Shoppe

Largo, FL See Page 30

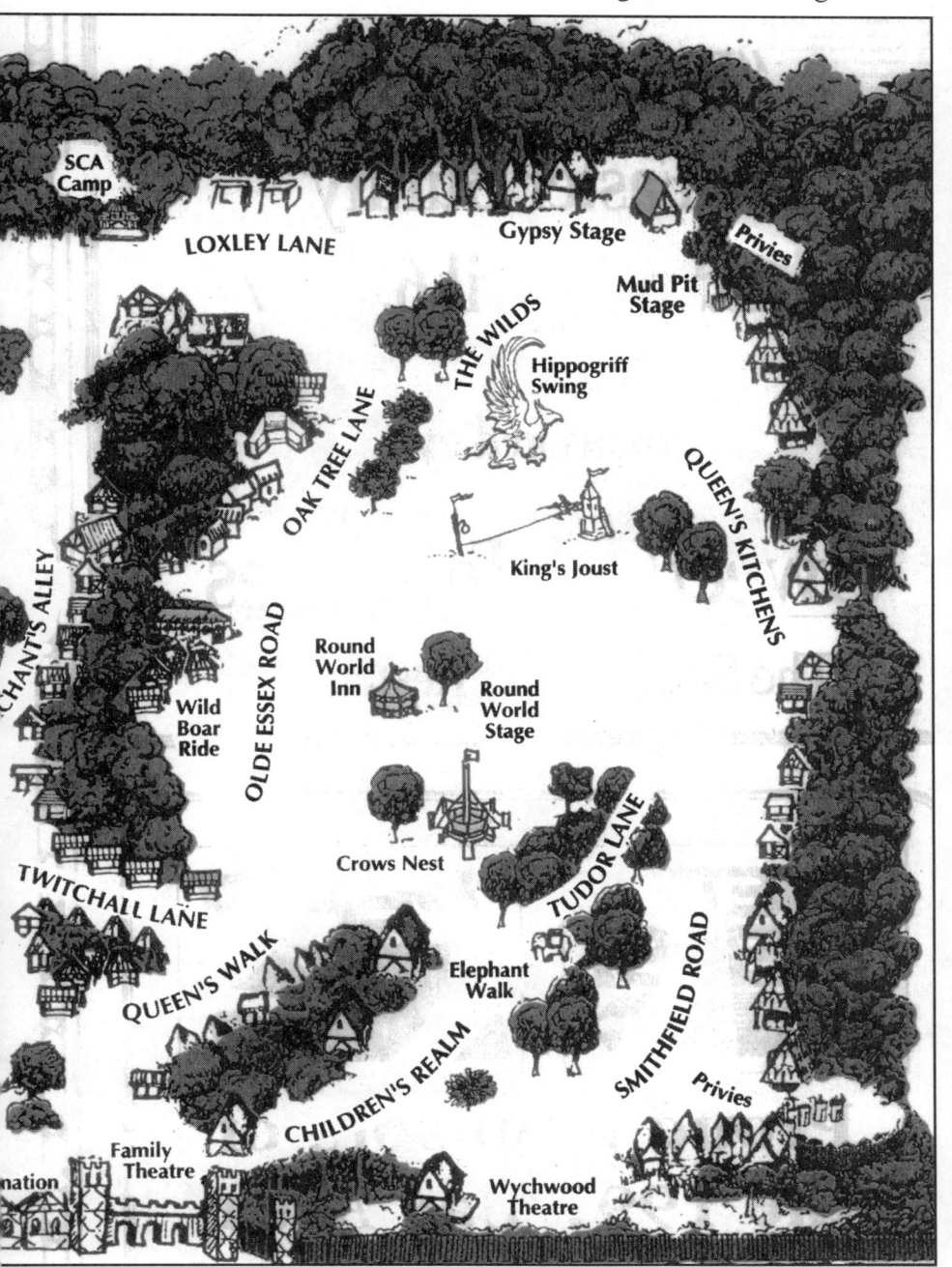

MICCOSUKEE INDIAN ARTS FESTIVAL
Since 1974
DEC - LAST FRI THRU JAN 1   ATTEND 20,000
Held on tribe's largest reservation (74,812) acres. My kind of party. It lasts ONE WEEK. Tribes from all over Continental Americas gather in unusual setting of "deep EVERGLADES". Indian culture is showcased via the arts. See Miccosukee doll and intricate beadwork, colorful Navajo sandpaintings and Cherokee moccasins.

MICCOSUKEE Fashion Show Features delicate Patchwork Clothing---See Authentic AZTEC Dancers From Mexico---Intertribal Singers & Dancers---Talented Mescalero APACHE Folk Singer---Renowned LAKOTA Flautist & Hoop Dancers---I Was In Awe At Vibrant Color "Handmade" Costumes & Lithesome Steps Of Groups Dancing To Drums & Songs Of Their Ancestors---Vast Array Of Indian Arts, Crafts (Outstanding Silver & Turquoise Jewelry)---Sweetgrass Baskets---Miccosukee FRY BREAD, PUMPKIN BREAD, SOFKEE & 'GATOR TAIL

Since this site is a permanent Misccosukee Reservation there are additional things to see in village.
- **Alligator Wrestling Pits**
- **Seamstress Demonstrations**
- **Miccosukee Museum Of Culture**
- **Airboat Rides Into The Glades**
- **Missosukee Restaurant Serving Indian & American Dishes**
- **Indian Village**

FACT: After third Seminole War (1855-1858) about 50 Miccosukee escaped to the Everglades, today their descendants number 550.

Miccosukee Indian Village   7 Day Festival   305-223-8380
25 Miles West Of Miami On Hwy 41   305-223-8388

MICCOSUKEE INDIAN VILLAGE
Florida Everglades

① MUSEUM   ③ ARTS & CRAFTS   ⑤ COOK CHICKEE   ⑦ GIFT SHOP
② SEWING   ④ NATIVE ISLAND   ⑥ ALLIGATOR WRESTLING   ⑧ VILLAGE

SEMINOLE ARTS & CRAFTS
Since 1938
MID - FEB ATTEND 12,000
Lovely new covered arena. Lodging in Okeechobee. Alligator wrestling. Seminole cultural village. Indian arts & crafts. Seminole garb contests. 4-H livestock sale. STANDOUT JEWELRY.

Authentic Indian Food---Traditional Indian Wrestling---RODEO (ALL INDIAN)---Vendors From All North America

Brighton Indian Reservation
South of Okeechobee Fl   Rd 721   3 Days   941-763-4128

SWAMP CABBAGE FESTIVAL
Since 1967
LATE FEB - WEEKEND ATTEND 15,000
Scenic site is on (high) banks of Caloosahatchee River under "senator" oaks in Barron Park. "Heart" of cabbage palm tree is main course. Parade & RODEO. CLOGGERS!!!

Colorful Indian Garb Sold---Seminole Foods ('licious pumpkin fry bread gator tail steak) Ribs & Swamp Cabbage Served Every Style---Native American Art & Crafts Sale---Music

Labelle Fl   3 Days   941-675-0125

SEMINOLE TRIBAL FAIR POW-WOW & PROFESSIONAL RODEO
Since 1970
FEB - 1ST WEEK ATTEND 15,000
Reservation (500) acres has 4 locations where events take place. The LIVING VILLAGE, STADIUM, RODEO ARENA & ALLIGATOR PIT. See weekend Canoe Race at Turnpike Lake.

Indian Archery Contest, Log Peeling, 12 Indian Product Booths ---Aztec Dancers---Panther & Snake Exhibits---ALLIGATOR WRESTLING---All Indian Professional Rodeo (10 Acre Shelter Arena) Lots Art, Crafts---Eat Fry-Bread, Alligator Tail (Both Yum-Yum)---HA-SHOU-BOU-SHO-CO-WA!!! I Hope The Sun Will Be Shining

Hollywood Fl   5 Days   954-967-3706
N.W. Corner Rd 7 (441) & Stirling Rd

SARASOTA JAZZ
Since 1980
MARCH - LAST WEEK   ATTEND 15,000
Star-studded jammin'. Rhythm & Blues. Jazz legends appear (Woody Herman & Count Basie Orchestras). Stage on "over-load" with old & new talent. Stride pianos bring sound of Harlem.

Hall (Great Acoustics)---Meet Musicians Reception---Jazz Club Jam---Jazz In Park (7 Hours)---Food Booths---Jazz On Bayfront (Free) Dogs Soft Drinks Beer---Tickets 941-953-3368

Sarasota Fl   Van Wezel Arts Hall   5 Days   941-366-1552

BLUEGRASS FEST
Since 1988
MARCH - MIDDLE WEEKEND   ATTEND 30,000
Pickin, fiddlin', dancin' at its best. Banjo specialists. Solo & Family Performers. NIGHT EVENTS.

Clogging Is A Sanctioned National Competition---Evening Concerts Are Outstanding "Jam Sessions"---Flea Market---Craft & Food Booths

Punta Gorda Fl   3 Days   941-639-2222

BLUEGRASS KISSIMMEE
Since 1977
MARCH - 1ST WEEKEND   ATTEND 6,000
A "magnitudinal" Kiwanis charity event. Toe-tappin' country struttin' beat music. Selected & recognized Southern groups.

Night Performances, too---Camping & Tenting Allowed---Some Covered Seating---Crafts Food & Beverage---1, 2, 3 Day Passes

Kissimmee Fl   3 Days   800-473-7773   407-856-0245
Silver Spurs Rodeo Grounds

INTERNATIONAL CARILLON FESTIVAL
Since 1980
FEB - 2ND WEEK   ATTEND 12,000
Carillon is a set of bells sounded by hammers of keyboard controls. Concert drifts from (53) BRONZE BELLS (biggest-11 tons, smallest-17 lbs). Concerts & recitals are "a rich-cultural experience", at Bok Tower (NATIONAL HISTORIC LANDMARK)

> *Outdoor Garden (157 Acres) Atop IRON MOUNTAIN (295 Feet) Lend Drama---Guest Carillonneurs From Several Nations---Seminars, Organ, Piano & Choral Concerts In Lake Wales---(1 Only) Breathtaking MOONLIGHT RECITAL!!!*

Lake Wales Fl   7 Days   941-676-9412
Bok Tower Gardens Hwy 27

HOLLYWOOD JAZZ
Since 1982
NOV - WEEKEND PRIOR THANKSGIVING   ATTEND 80,000
Outdoors at roomy Young Circle Park. Evening & afternoon performances, VIP & 3-day bandshell passes or day ticket.

> *Only The Greats Appear---Fest Is 1 of Top 10 Of WORLD JAZZ CONCERTS, Solos, Trios, Quartets, Quintets Groups ---Taste Of Hollywood Plus Arts & Crafts---Join The "Circle" & Groove With The Masters*

Hollywood Fl   Young Circle Park   3 Days   954-923-4000

RIVERWALK BLUES
Since 1986
NOV - 2ND WEEKEND   ATTEND 90,000
Along Lauderdale's "gorgeous" New River on mile-long promenade. Green Bubier Park makes perfect backdrop. Admire passing water-taxi's & luxury yachts. Varied array of vendors fans out to many side streets.

> *6 Stages---National Acts---Lecture Venue---LEGENDS Perform On "Sound Advice" Stage---Attendant Concert Locations*

Ft Lauderdale Downtown   3 Days   954-462-6000
New River   Bubier Park

FALL FEST
Since 1996
NOV - WEEKEND CLOSEST VETERAN'S DAY
ATTEND 30,000

Outdoor Autumn atmosphere of C.B. Smith Park adds to your pleasure. Woody greens boast 60 acres of lakes. Activities run into night hours. Miramar-Pembroke Pines Chamber sponsors the event with main focus on families and there are "droves" of them in attendance. Drawings for prizes. Entrance fee is "miniscule" because of CORPORATE SPONSOR participation.

Adults & Young-'uns both toe-tap to CONTINUOUS MUSIC---Jazz, Oldies, Swing, Latin, Country---Local Featured Artists---Harmony Singing, Flamenco Dances, Ballet Folkloric---Full Carnival (30) Rides, Bounce House & Pony Rides---Karate & THEATRE PRODUCTIONS for "kiddies"---Plus (50) Arts, Craft Booths---Extensive Choice Food Purveyors

Pembroke Pines Fl   3 Days   954-432-9808
C.B. Smith Park 900 Flamingo Rd

FLORIDA STATE CHAMPIONSHIP BLUEGRASS FESTIVAL
Since 1971

MARCH - 3RD WEEKEND   ATTEND 100,000

"Pickin" site is 32 acres on grounds of one of state's largest flea markets. There's even a Pickin' Parlour in the market cafe. Creative masters of the guitar, banjo, mandolin, fiddle, bass and dobro perform. They hail from all over the southeast and Florida, too. You can browse the undercover 800 vendor flea mart and still hear the bluegrass bands.

Biggest Bluegrass Gathering In Florida---Overnight Camping Facilities---2 Stages---Competitions---Night Performances & Day---Plaza Food Court---Dancers & Cloggers---Bring Lawn Chairs

Auburndale Fl   1052 Hwy 92 West   3 Days   941-665-0062

ARCADIA RODEO
Since 1929

EACH MARCH & JULY   ATTEND 19,000

Its' the "granddaddy" championship RO-DAY-O of 'em all! Professional cowboys battle for points and prize money. Covered arena with good viewing.

Downtown Parade Train Robbery & Shoot-Outs---Bull Riding (Everyone's Favorite)---Buckin' Pitchin' Twirlin' BRONCO RIDES ---Highly Skilled QUADRILLE (Horse & Rider Square Dance)!---Calf Roping---Barrel Races---Bareback---Noon Bar B. Q. m-m-m-m-m

Arcadia Fl   3 Days   800-749-7633 or 941-494-2014

ORANGE BLOSSOM STATE CHAMPIONSHIP PRO RODEO
Since 1940

NOV - WEEKEND BEFORE THANKSGIVING ATTEND 15,000

Local community has roots & traditions in rodeoing spanning many generations. Davie rodeo was initiated by country "boys" & farm families. Today it is the last pro event for ranking prior to December NATIONAL FINALS in Las Vegas, Nev.

This is Riding With The Big Boys & Healthiest STOCK Available---250 Entrants From Southeast U.S.---Covered Arena & Seating For 10,000---Saddle, Bareback, Bronc, Bull Ride Events & Much More---Important Score Points: Toes Must Be Turned Out On Leaving Chute. Not Touch Horse Saddle Or Self With Free Hand. 64 Average 78 Superior 80 Plus Outstanding---Yes, Animals Are Scored Too! High Jumpers Are Spectacular But High Kickers Make Harder Rides. Spinning Animals Get More Points Then Bucking Ones. Mounts That "SUNFISH" (Show Their Belly) Are Real STARS & Often Cause The Cowboys To "See-Them"!!!

Davie Cooper City Fl   Bergeron Arena   3 Days   954-581-0790

WESTFAIR-BIGGEST RODEO IN THE EAST
Since 1995
FEB - LAST WEEKEND THROUGH 1ST WEEK MARCH
ATTEND 60,000

Held in the only U.S. city boasting a McDONALD'S DRIVE-THRU WITH HORSEBACK ACCESS!!! 10 event packed days in a town with visible western heritage & flair. Rodeo is part of "Orange Blossom Festival in its 61st year.

300 Cowboys, Cowgirls Participate From U.S. Canada & Brazil---6 Scored Events---Purse Over $110,000---Covered Arena On 30 Acres (Seats 7,000)---Music Concerts By Western Superstars---Gigantic Midway & Carnival Rides---Plenty Western Vendor Booths---Couple Of Facts For "City Slickers": Snappy Horse (Bucks 8 to 13 Times) In 8 Seconds And For Points Riders Must Stay On Mounts For 8 Seconds!

David Cooper City Fl   10 Days   954-581-0790
Bergeron Arena-Orange Dr

FLORIDA "CRACKER" TRAIL RIDE
Since 1987
MARCH - 1ST WEEK

Re-enacts cattle drive route from west to east coast. From Bradenton to Ft Pierce on backroads through ranchlands & historic sites (Fort Bassinger & Lockett ranch house).

150 Riders---Wagon Train---Chuck Wagon & Night Campouts---20 Miles Daily---Spectator Viewing On Hwys. 64, 66, 98 & 68---Neat Roads For Photogs

Bradenton Fl   7 Days   941-385-5036

SEAFOOD FEST
Since 1988
FEB - 2ND WEEKEND   ATTEND 40,000
Nautical backdrop of passing yachts in Intracoastal Waterway. Currie Park spills over with canopy booths offering "bounty of the sea", Noon & NIGHT event.

Fare Is Baked, Buttered, Battered & Delicious---Taste Pink Shrimp, Sweet Scallops, Fish, Chowders, Gumbos, Complete Dinners Too!---Original Crafts For Sale

West Palm Beach Fl   3 Days   561-833-3711
Flagler Dr. Currie Park

JOHN'S PASS SEAFOOD FESTIVAL
Since 1979
OCT - NEXT TO LAST WEEKEND   ATTEND 100,000
Site overlooks emerald Gulf & quaint mercantile village on I.C.W. Cruise ships (4 story) dockside. Streets flow with SEAFARE (to drool for).

Scores Of Restaurants (Crabs, Oyster, Creamy Gumbo, Scallops, Plump Pink Shrimp)!!---Fireworks--Stage Shows---An Outdoor Rollicking Event---Art & Crafts

Madeira Beach Fl   At John's Pass   3 Days   813-821-4069

RUSKIN SEAFOOD & ARTS
Since 1988
NOV - 1ST WEEKEND   ATTEND 10,000
Down a less traveled road to 458 acre E.G. SIMMONS PARK on Tampa Bay. Boat show is a "draw". Children's Court (face paint, magic, puppets, pet zoo).

Fresh Clam, Grilled Seafood, Grouper, Smoked Mullet, Crab Rolls & More---Cloggers Steel Drums Blues & Country---Arts Craft Booths---Park Has R.V. & Camping Facilities

Ruskin Fl   E.G. Simmons Park   2 Days   813-645-3808

GRANT SEAFOOD FESTIVAL
Since 1966

FEB - 3RD WEEKEND   ATTEND 70,000

Following is the shopping list for Grant's marine feast:

- 20,000 Clams
- 600 Gallons Oysters
- 3,500 Lbs Fish Fillets
- 550 Lbs Crab Meat
- 1,200 Lbs Steamed Shrimp
- 1,500 Lbs Scallops
- 1,600 Lbs Fried Shrimp
- 250 Gallons Clam Chowder
    (Made on premises)
- 7,000 Lbs Cooking Oil
- 4,000 Lbs Flour & Corn Meal
- 550 Lbs Linguine Pasta
- 80 Lbs Baking Powder
- 200 Gallons Buttermilk
- 700 Gallons Pork & Beans
- 2,500 Lbs Cole Slaw
    AND
- 3,000 Lbs French Fries

Guess they shop with an "18 wheeler semi"!!!

And Grant is a small riverside town of only 2,700 people!!! Stroll the grounds to admire work of 65 crafters original items. Convenient on-site parking. Full dinners are served along with A "LA CARTE booths with modest prices. All day live entertainment. Choice of beverages (icy-beer too) to ease down those delicious seafood plates.

Grant Fl   2 Days   407-723-8687
Community Center Grounds U.S. Hwy 1

EVERGLADES SEAFOOD FESTIVAL
Since 1973

FEB - 1ST FULL WEEKEND   ATTEND 65,000

Town canals are lined with crab-pots and fishing skiffs. Generations of families have made their livelihood from local waters flowing through these "10,000 islands".

Menu Goodies Are: Stone Crab Claws, Gator Nuggets, Cajun Seafood, Creamy Gumbo, Shrimp, Fried Fish, INDIAN FRY BREAD & Trimmings Galore---150 Craft Booths---Indian Tribes In Colorful Garb Sell Native Crafts---Kiddie Carnival Rides Continuous Live Music---Poke Around Everglades City. Its' A Remnant Of "By-Gone Era"!!!

Everglades City Fl Town Park Hwy 29 3 Days 941-695-4100

SHARKS TOOTH & SEAFOOD FEST
Since 1990
AUGUST - 2ND WEEKEND   ATTEND 45,000

Sharks have 7 rows of teeth. In 10 yrs. Tiger Shark produce 24,000 teeth. Waves & tides at VENICE BEACHES uncover uncountable fossil teeth each year!

Display & Collector's Tent---Fossils to 35 Million Yrs---One Of Top 250 Events In U.S.---Kids SHARK-A-MANIA ---Sea Turtle Exhibits---Sand Castle Contest---Beach & Fish Pier (720 Ft)Nearby---Delicious Seafood Booths Galore

Venice Fl   2 Days   800-940-7427 Or 941-488-2236

BOYNTON BEACH G.A.L.A.
Since 1981
MARCH - 1ST WEEKEND   ATTEND 40,000

This is a top quality event with a multitude of cultural happenings. G.A.L.A. stands for (Great American Love Affair) as it melds the arts, entertainments, business and cultural groups together. Each year brings many innovations to the gathering. Setting of pretty downtown Boynton Beach adds fanfare and a large brightly colored festival tents also lend flair.

Nationally Known Acts Appear---Continuous Entertainment In (4) Staging Areas---A Most Varied Food Court---More Than 200 Fine Artists and Crafter From Many States---Refreshing Beer And Wine Garden---Kids Corner Sports Games & Rides---Screening Committee For Arts & Crafts Prize Competitions---Unusual "HOMESPUN MARKETPLACE"---Charming and Original Youth Art Exhibit (600) Pieces

Boynton Beach Fl   3 Days   561-732-9501
Ocean Ave & Federal Hwy

Venice Sharks Tooth & Seafood Festival

You Can Find These On Our Beaches

MAKO   BULL   TIGER   LEMON

EXTINCT MAKO   SAND SHARK   DUSKY   CARCHARDON

SANIBEL SHELL FAIR
Since 1937
MARCH - 1ST WEEK   ATTEND 50,000

Takes place on island "famed" for shelling! Held in white clapboard landmark built in 1927. Over 35 shell divisions exhibited. Fossils, too.

Creative Shell Artwork---Trophys, Awards, Prizes---Top Shell Show in U.S.---Visit BAILEY MATTHEWS SHELL MUSEUM On Island!!!

Sanibel Island Fl   4 Days   941-472-2155

LIGHTHOUSE GALLERY FINE ART FESTIVAL
Since 1963
NOV - WEEKEND PRIOR THANKSGIVING   ATTEND 10,000

Seaside ambiance in Atlantic Oceanside Carlin Park. A rich pool of talent limited to 160 artists to maintain quality & excellence. Good parking. LARGE DISPLAY AREA. Outdoor Beachside.

All Work Original---Artists Must Personally Exhibit---Juried Show---Broad Spectrum (15 Media)---See Historic Jupiter Lighthouse

Jupiter Fl   2 Days   561-746-3101

SANDSCULPTING FESTIVAL
Since 1986
OCT - LAST WEEKEND   ATTEND 20,000

A marvy excuse to play in the sand! Contest is actually sophisticated. Tools are masonry, garden, tampers, shovels, buckets & 1 WHEELBARROW & 1 LADDER.

Categories Are Amateur, Master And Group (5 Arteeests) Per Team---Work Area (10'x10')---Arts-N-Crafts---Fest Is A "Sand"-BLAST!!!---Tote Camera

Ft Myers Beach Fl   Front Beach Of Outrigger Resort & Holiday Inn   2 Days   941-454-7500

INTERNATIONAL FILM FESTIVAL
Since 1985
NOV - 1ST 12 DAYS   ATTEND 55,000

Sensational global cinema. Draws European fans & industry pro's. Educational seminars on technology production, music, writing, distribution, CHILDREN'S MINI FEST.

150 Screenings---Nine Locations---Scores Of Independent Films From 30 Countries---Special Opening & Closing Night Films---WRAP PARTY---11 Celebrity Galas

Ft Lauderdale Fl   12 Days   800-745-4621 Or 954-564-7373

FLORIDA WINEFEST
Since 1990
APRIL - LAST WEEK   ATTEND 11,000

Superb forum for wine & food. Tropical setting on LONGBOAT KEY. Sample 80 top vintners creations. Renowned chefs prepare gourmet menus.

Taste Florida, Collector, U.S. & International Wine Flavors---Seminars---Showcase Luncheon & Dinners---Cooperage Demo (Barrel Making)---Late Night Cognacs & Cigars.

Longboat Key Fl   4 Days   941-952-1109

FOOD & WINE APPRECIATION WEEKEND
Since 1991
AUG - EARLY WEEKEND   ATTEND 500

For the "bon vivant"! Champagne brunches, extravagant dinners, "smokers" with cigars, cognac & port. An epicurean tradition with DELUXE rooms for (2) evenings. Cooking demos & seminars.

Held In 1926 Historic & Opulent BOCA RATON RESORT & CLUB---Event Is Melange Of Cooking Styles & Flavors Distilled Into A "Taster's Nirvana" GRAND DINNER In The Vineyard Is Prepared By (6) Select CHEFS. I Wonder How "Kitchen Etiquette" fares that night???

Boca Raton Fl   Open To Guests & Members Only Boca Raton Resort & Club   2 Days   800-327-0101   561-395-3000

GASPARILLA PIRATE FEST
Since 1904
FEB - 1ST WEEKEND   ATTEND 400,000

Nearly 100 years old, fest is ranked in top 100 in U.S.A.!! Sails billowing flags flying cannons booming & pistols blazing hundreds of pirates aboard pirate ship JOSE GASPARILLA sail up the channel & take over "Tampa town streets" for 3 days of merriment. Friday warm-up is full of big name music, street dancing, tummy fillers & LASER LIGHT SHOW.

Fireworks Show---Pirate Themed Art & Crafts---A Sat. PARADE OF PIRATES Features Stunning Floats Stirring Bands & Ye Mystic Krewes---Vintage Car Race (St Augustine To Tampa)---Pirate Pandemonium Reigns For 3 Days---Midway Rides

Tampa Fl   Downtown Streets & Parks   3 Days   813-353-8070

RIVER DAYZ & SEAFOOD SAMPLER
Since 1994
NOV - WEEKEND PRIOR THANKSGIVING   ATTEND 12,000

Celebrates giving restored life to 30 mile long St Lucie River. On waterfront in historic downtown Stuart. Flagler Park becomes a native village with Creek Indian emcampment & demos. Meet authentic Medicine Man from South America.

Giant Sand Sculpture (15 Tons Sand) Riverlife Theme---Pirate Encounter & Ooze Cruise---Native American Group Sing, Dance In Pow-Wow Dress---Creations In Oils Glass Wood Clay & Metals---Top Name Singers & Bands---An "Aurora Borealis" Of Sizziling Seafood Dishes

Stuart Fl   2 Days   561-287-1088

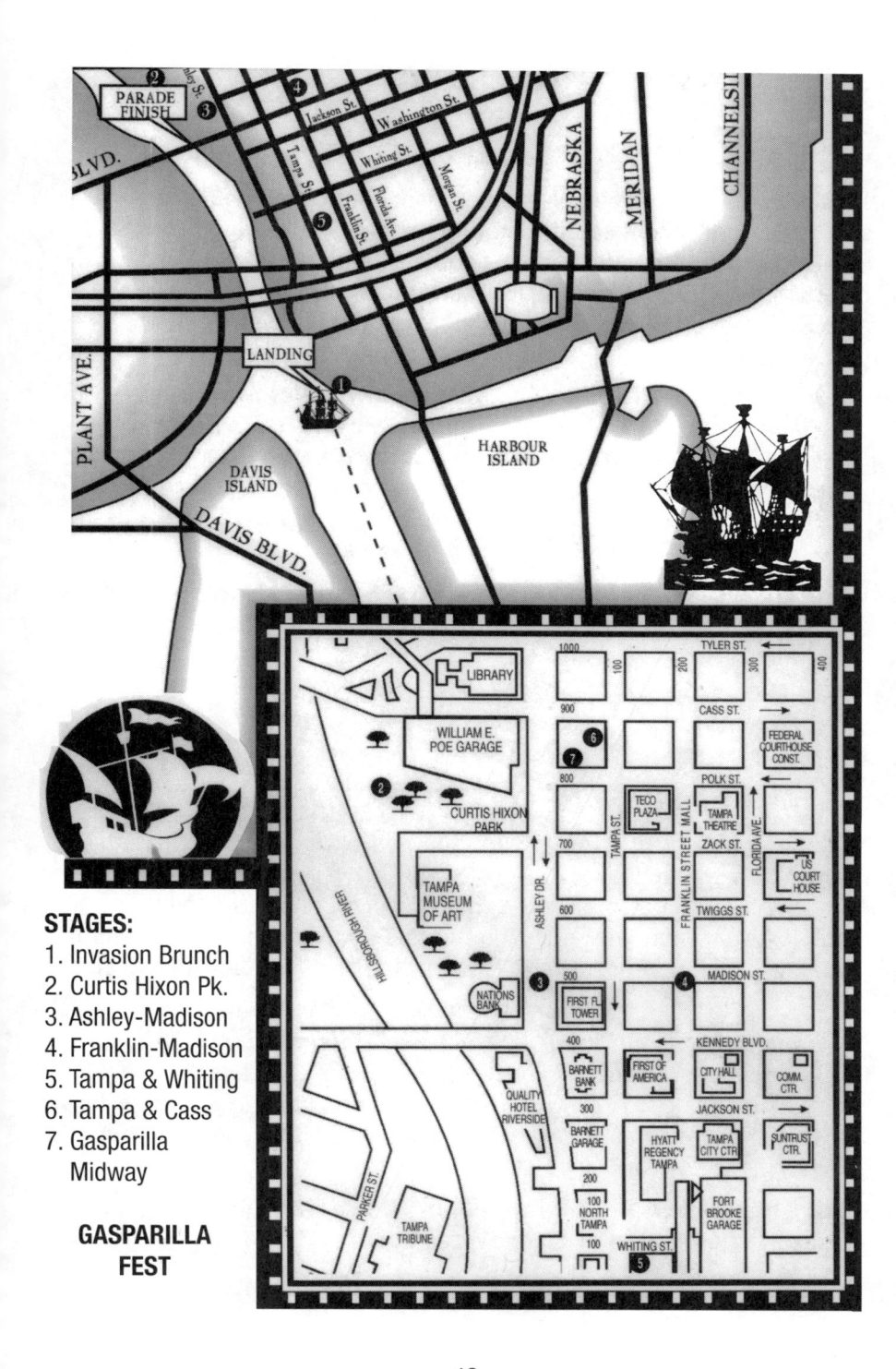

STAGES:
1. Invasion Brunch
2. Curtis Hixon Pk.
3. Ashley-Madison
4. Franklin-Madison
5. Tampa & Whiting
6. Tampa & Cass
7. Gasparilla Midway

GASPARILLA FEST

49

GOOMBAY
Since 1976
JUNE - 1ST WEEKEND   ATTEND 550,000
Held along shores of lovely tropical Coconut Grove!!! Savor atmosphere of the Bahamas. Fest honors south Florida's first black settlers with Bahamian roots in 1800's. Junkanoo (music) groups dance down Grand Ave (transformed into NASSAU'S BAY STREET) for weekend. Island rhythms come from cowbells, drums, whistles to rake-n-scrape instruments.

Royal Bahamas Band (British African) Styles March By---Spectators Join Revelry As Junkanoo Shakes By---400 Vendors---Native Dishes Offer Bahamian Chowder, Cracked Conch & More Caribbean Treats---Costumes & Island Dress Provide A Riot Of Moving Color On FESTIVAL STREET---3 Music Stages---Marvelous Family Event

Coconut Grove Fl   3 Days   305-444-7270

SUNSETS AT PIER 60
Since 1993
YEAR ROUND - THURS THRU MON - 2 HRS PRIOR & 2 HRS AFTER SUNSET   ATTEND 700 - 1,000 NIGHTLY
Wide long pier jutting into green Gulf of Mexico waters. Sort of resembles a gussied-up floating flea market. Twinkling boat lights on horizon vie with glittery beach glow along shoreline. Neither comes close to matching the rich hues & tints splashed across night skies by THE OLD MASTER PAINTER!!! Setting is just right for evening "carnival" atmosphere.

Each Night Is Different---Street Performers, Mimes, Talented Musicians---Unusual Handcrafted Goods---Artists ---Entrance On Pier Is F-R-E-E---Case Adjacent Avenues & Wharves For Food-N-Bevs---Neat Family Entertainment & Jolly Way To End Your Day

Clearwater Beach Fl Nightly (Thurs Thru Mon) 813-461-0011
West of Rd 60 North of Clearwater Pass

POKER RUN
Since 1972
SEPT - 3RD WEEKEND   ATTEND 20,000

Appeared to me like a gigantic bash-mix of "bingo, bikin' & braggin'. Thousands of powerful MOTORCYCLES surge through streets. Glittzy bikes are everywhere (admire but not touch)! Friendly bikers "shop-talk" with non-riders too. To play POKER RUN you don't have to ride a motorcycle . . . . just buy poker sheets, have'em stamp at check-in around town & keep fingers crossed.

Bike Show Memory Lane---Prizes & Bike Raffle---Tattoo Contest (Quite Imaginative)---Blessing Of The Bikes (Mallory Square)---Welcome Party---Music (Downtown Streets Of Key West)---Best Part Of Festival Is In-The-Streets---Poker Run Is A CHARITY EVENT & Baskets Of Fun

Key West Fl   3 Days   800-527-8539   305-294-2587

C.C.C. FESTIVAL
Since 1985
NOV - 1ST SAT   ATTEND 3,000

Young men of the Civilian Conservation Corps built Florida's first state parks. In 1930's they made roads trails cabins & bridges sending home their pay while living in barracks. Held in "gorgeous" 5,000 acre Highland Hammock State Park!

Still Existing Are Bailey's Camp Store C.C.C. MUSEUM (Top-Notch), Cabins & Trails---Folk Music, Craft Demos, Clogging, Animal Exhibits---Smoked Barbecue Dishes

Sebring Fl   Highland Hammock   1 Day   941-386-6094

C.C.C. THE FIRST 10 YEARS 1931-1941

Young people ages (17-25) enrolled.
Paid $35 monthly.
Their legacy to Florida:
  Planted 19,000,000 trees.
  Cleared 3,700 miles of trails.
  Built 2,750 bridges

Developed 8 state parks.
Highland Hammock-Sebring
Myakka River - Sarasota
Hillsboro River - Tampa
Gold Head - Keystone Heights
O'Leno-High Springs
Ft Clinch-Fernandina
Torreya-Bristol
Florida Caverns - Marianna

INTERNATIONAL PAVILION ON-THE-WATERWAY

If only event here was a "caterpillar crawl", I would attend because of the "GORGEOUSITY" of setting! 45,000 sq ft pavilion is a poly-flex moveable structure. Each "put-up, take-down" costs $800,000. Pavilion is up for 4 months in Winter. Site is on curve jutting into I.C.W. (busy with yachts).

INTERNATIONAL ART & ANTIQUE FAIR
Since 1996
JAN - LAST WEEK & FEB - 1ST WEEK (10 DAYS) ATTEND 30,000

60 of world's renowned dealers. Elaborate showing installations.

SOTHEBY Exhibits---Master Paintings---Silver, Jewelry Antiquities---Collector Furniture & Other Objets d'art

ART & DESIGN FAIR
Since 1996
MARCH - 2ND WEEK (4 DAYS)   ATTEND 20,000

70 prestigious dealers. Works are contemporary. Perfect show venue as 23% of WORLD'S WEALTHY gather in (south Florida) each Winter!

I Was Impressed With Innovative Flair Of Works---Glass, Fine Art, Furniture & So-o-o-o Much More---Attendees Come To BUY, To Be SEEN & To Make A Culture STATEMENT!--- Groups Welcome (Discounts)---Normal Arrival Is By Car & Bus But There Is YACHT DOCKAGE!!!

INTERNATIONAL FOOD & WINE FAIR
Since 1996
FEB - LAST WEEKEND (3 DAYS)   ATTEND 5,000

Epitome of style & elegance---Evening Galas

300 World Wide Vintners, Gourmet Food Purveyors, Distillers- --Vast Array Of Tastings, Seminars, Culinary Presentations

Palm Beach Fl   3 Fairs Listed Above   **561-220-2690**
P.B. Intnl. Pavilion (Consumers Welcome) At Clematis On Intercoastal Waterway

SUNFEST
Since 1982
WED - BEFORE 1ST WEEKEND IN MAY (5 DAYS) ATTEND 300,000

3,000 volunteers are responsible for the L-A-R-G-E-S-T music, art, waterfront festival in state!!! Fest has location, location, location!!! (On yacht filled lagoon of I.C.W.) Features musicians of "national stature". Extends to night hours.

> *Waterfront GATE For Boats---40 Concerts (5) Stages--- Four Fabulous Food Courts---Inexpensive SAMPLER Program Is Delicious---Floating Oasis Are (2) Barges Serving Tropical Drinks, Snacks, Entertainment---"Brita Lagoon" Has Pedalboat Rentals & Illuminated Fountains ---Market Place Artisans & Fine Art Show (350)---Riotous Fireworks Display---This Is A STELLAR WATERFRONT BLOWOUT.... I Could Tell 'Cause Volunteers Were Having As Much Fun As Anybody*

West Palm Beach Fl   5 Days   **561-833-3711**
Flagler Dr On (I.C.W.)

PUMPKIN FESTIVAL
Since 1992
LATE OCT - WEEKEND   ATTEND 40,000

90 Acre pumpkin farm. 2 red barns (mercantile & feed). Boogie barn stage. PIONEER TRADE VILLAGE. Hay rides & walk-in corn stalk "maze".

> *150 Craft Booths---Barnyard Zoo, Kid Games---Vittles Galore (Punkin' Pie, Cider, Hot Corn etc.)---Oak Grove Canopy---Year Round U-PICK Hotline (Veggies, Berries) & PRIVATE PARTIES (10-3000 Folks)---Scale Of 1 To 10, I Rate This Fest A 99!*

Hunsader Farms Sarasota Fl
St Rd 70 To Rd 675 - 4 Miles North   3 Days   **941-322-2168**

FELLSMERE FROGLEG FESTIVAL
Since 1991
JAN - 3RD WEEK - THURS, FRI, SAT, SUN
ATTEND 55,000

Fellsmere is in "boonies" near lots of wetlands, so hopper-frogs are a-plenty. A few historic strutures stand beside old 1910 streets. Hamlet was settled by Englishman, E.A. Fell who was an international mining engineer and served the Czar of Russia. How amazed he'd be today to discover his town is famed for T-shirts labeled: LEGS-R-US & KISS MY FROG!!!!

Fest Kicks Off With Cajun Music, Comedy Acts & Of Course Frog-Calling (Rrrrrbit)---Lots Entertainment Includes Sunset Skydive Jumps, Variety Of Music---Weekend Features Country, Bluegrass & Gospel Nights---Natch, Main Attraction All 4 Days Is Deep Fried Frog Legs, Cole Slaw, Hush Puppies & Grits---Yes, Froglegs, May Be Purchased By The Pound & Yes, I've Eaten Them & Yes, They're Yummy---Arts & Crafts Area SPECTACULAR M-I-D-W-A-Y (Adult & Kid Rides)

Fellsmere Fl   **4 Days**   **561-571-0008**
Rd 512 N.W. Of Vero Beach

OTHER ODD FLORIDA FESTS

WORM FIDDLING FEST - September - Caryville

BOGGY BAYOU MULLET - October - Niceville 250,000 Attend - 800-322-3319

PEANUTS - October - Williston - Since 1988

ANYTHING THATS FLOATS RIVER RAFT RACE - September - Deland - 904-734-3495

ALLIGATOR FEST - May - Lake City - Since 1992

PEPPER FESTIVAL - May - Webster - Since 1991

CANE GRINDING - Feb - Ortuna - Since 1989 941-946-0440

MARDI GRAS LAKE WALES
Since 1985
FEB - SAT SUN PRIOR TO FAT TUESDAY LATE FEB
ATTEND 55,000

Laissez les bon temps rouler . . . . Let the good times roll . . . . and they do for 2 weeks! Here are some KREWES participating & their names suggest what carnival is all about: Mystical Krewe of Oomphos Bacchus, Mystic Krewe of Maunder, Les Jolies Dames, Krewe of Zombies, Krewe of Flocking Flamingos and other wild groups. New Orleans style P-A-R-A-D-E on Saturday is an outdoor roaring "gala" flowing through historic downtown.

Jazz Greats Appear---Dixieland Jazz, Big Band Swing & Rock-N-Roll Are Belted Out---Sassy Vibrant Floats---Rougish Flamboyant COSTUMES---Downtown Market Place Is Staging Area---SERIOUS POST-PARADE PARTY (In Town Streets)---Many Spectators Attend In Costume---All Krewe Parties & Mardi Gras Events Are Open To The Public---For Flakey Florida Fun This Fest Is "Tops"!!!

Lake Wales Fl   2 Days   941-676-3445
Downtown Streets

SARASOTA
SAILOR CIRCUS
The Greatest Little Show On Earth

Practice Open To Public
October Thru December
January Thru March
Call For Times

• **MUSEUM ON GROUNDS**

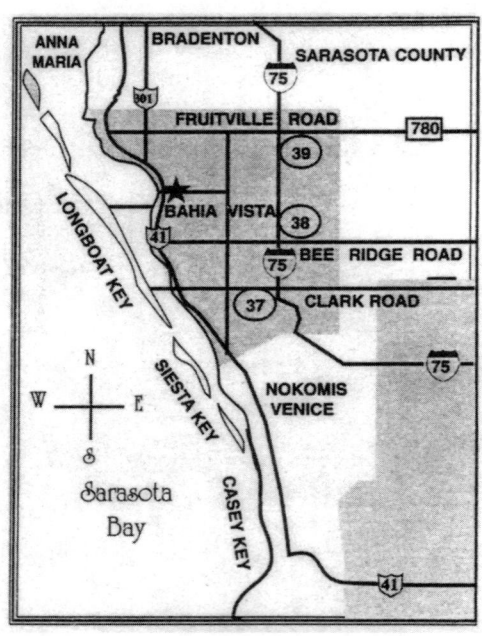

SAILOR CIRCUS
Since 1949

MAR - LAST WEEK & APRIL - 1ST WEEK   ATTEND 25,000

Actual CLASS act as performers are kidfolks in 3rd to 12th grades. Circus is an extra curricular program of Sarasota Schools run just like football. Some families have 4 generations of performers. Almost 500 volunteers get the acts "up in the air" from riggers to seamstresses who stitch on 5,000 costumes. Why called Sailor Circus!!! In 1920's Sarasota High School football, basketball, baseball teams competed with St Pete & Tampa. There were no good bridges or roads so teams sailed over on ferry boats and were always hailed as "Here come the "sailors"!!! Like any "big-top" circus the "sailors" have their own BLUE & WHITE DOMED PERMANENT FACILITY on 10 acres of land . . . . this is where practice, practice, practice makes perfect!

Skilled Trapeze Artists---Daring Aerial Feats---Double Somersaults (30 Ft In The Air)---90 Piece Band With All The Right Sounds---Over 5,000 Youngsters Have Gone Through This Program---Clowns & Rolling Globes---115 PERFORMERS---Glitzy Costumes & Thrilling Hi-Wire Acts---Teeterboard Titans, Perch Pole Pro's---Unicycle, Bicycling & Jugglers---Intermission For Hot Dogs, Popcorn, Cotton Candy---23 Stellar Acts ---Sailor Circus Has INTERNATIONAL REPUTATION Having Performed In Kyushu, Japan, Alaska, Lima, Peru & 25 States In U.S.A. & Macy's Thanksgiving Day Parade

Sarasota Fl   10 Days   941-361-6350
Corner U.S. 41 & Bahia Vista St (Nights & Matinees)

PIONEER PARK DAYS
Since 1968
MARCH - 1ST WEEK   ATTEND 100,000

Theme is "Old Time Country Fair" Pastoral setting hugs Peace River. 100's of R.V.'s at event. See Cracker Trail Museum. Savory international food tents.

> *Zoo On Grounds---Antique Engine & Car Show---Humongous Flea Mart---Cloggers Music Daily Entertainment---115 Acre Park Has Canoe Launch & Waterside Picnicking*

Zolfo Springs Fl   5 Days   941-773-2161   Park 941-735-0330

RATTLESNAKE FESTIVAL
Since 1967
OCT - 3RD SATURDAY   ATTEND 25,000

Event occurs in "post-card-pretty" City Park. Old time buildings ring the square! Highlight is Snakes Alive Show (fee, about 45 mins.) Select meats grilled on Bar-B-Q's.

> *Trade Skills Demos---Gopher Races---Impressive Quality Crafters---Pony Rides, Barn Critters---All Day Entertainment ---Year-Round Lunching At Charming SAN ANN MARKET RESTAURANT!!!*

San Antonio Fl   Historic Village   1 Day   352-588-4444

MELBOURNE HARBOR FESTIVAL
Since 1994
NOV - WEEKEND PRIOR THANKSGIVING   ATTEND 15,000

Neat waterside spot with lots going on! Crane Creek Promenade is a spiffy creek park with look overs for viewing slow-poke MANATEE who frequently visit.

> *Happening Celebrates Diversity Of INDIAN RIVER Which Isn't Really A River. It Is A 156 Mile LAGOON---Fest Choices Include Boat Show, Art Show---Business & Marine Marketplace---Marine Ed Exhibits---Local Seafood Sampling ---CANOE RACES---Entertainment Stages*

Melbourne Fl   Crane Creek Promenade   2 Days   407-724-5400

QUILT & ANTIQUE SHOW
Since 1990
FEB - 1ST WEEKEND   ATTEND 3,000

At historic Pioneer Fl Museum on 20 acre wooded hillside. This weekend quilters statewide hang up signs . . . ."GONE STITCHIN" . . . .

Displayed In 7 Historic Buildings On Grounds---Overstreet House Dates To 1860---Use Gloves To Admire Historic, New & Original Quilts Hanging Everywhere---Sales & Demos---Varied Array Antiques

Dade City Fl   Pioneer Fl Museum   2 Days   352-567-0262

ART DECO WEEKEND
Since 1978
JAN - 3RD WEEK   ATTEND 400,000

Salute to architecture & fashions of 1930's. Tram, walk, bike tours of "Deco Area" listed in National Register Of Historic Places. A week-long celebration. Area fronts on Atlantic Ocean. LINCOLN RD has finest and most exotic examples of Tropical Art Deco. SPANISH VILLAGE (Española Way) was designed for 1920's bohemian types. GROUP TOURS can be booked.

800 Buildings (Mediterranean Revival & Art Deco) Built Between 1923-1942---Unusual Design Is "Nautical Flair" Imitates Features Of Grand Ocean Liners Of 20's & 30's ---Brisk Buying At STREET FESTIVAL & Shoppes Showcasing Works Of The Era---Sidewalk Cafes, Street Theater, Lummus Park (Entertainment Stages)

Miami Beach Fl   4 Days   305-672-2014
Ar Deco Welcome Center (1001 Ocean Dr)

FANTASY FEST
Since 1977

OCT - WEEK BEFORE LAST ATTEND 100,000

America's top masked costume party. Totally "unplugged" 10 day celebration. Of what?? Who Cares?? Non-stop street fairs, masquerades, Goombay Days, Balls, Toga Parties. Best O-U-T-L-A-N-D-I-S-H event anywhere.

Caribbean Carnival Revelry Reigns!!!!!

Key West Fl   Everywhere On Island   4 Days   305-294-2587

MARATHON KEY FESTIVALS

- ▶ RENAISSANCE FAIRE – January (Mid)
- ▶ PIGEON KEY ART– (Historic Grounds) Feb – 1st Weekend
- ▶ MARATHON SEAFOOD FEST – March Last Weekend
- ▶ PIRATES IN PARADISE – May 1st Weekend

800-842-9580   305-743-5417

FANTASY FEST BEAUTIES

IRISH FEST
Since 1986
FEB - 2ND WEEKEND   ATTEND 55,000

The Irish have no reputation for bashfulness. In the lively event their playful nature and humorous antics are displayed "right-up-front". Setting is in Bubier Park beside waters of famous NEW RIVER riverwalk. Attendees must have a love for all things IRISH and pull out all "stops" for having f-u-n!!! Heritage & rock bands from Ireland perform. Food vendors serve favorite Irish "beverages" for TOASTING anything & everyone including Irish heros like John Barry, "Father Of The U.S. Navy Charles Carroll, signer of Declaration Of Independence and outlaw Billy the Kid (born Henry Mcarty)!

> *3 Stages---Irish Stepdancing Groups (No Upper Body Movement)---30 Bands---Celtic Rock Night (Fri Night)---Precision Bagpipers---Sunday Mass In GAELIC---Irish Marketplace With Many Celtic Crafters---Irish & Traditional Cuisine Food Plazas---Night Events---Event Is Largest Irish Festival In Southeast United States!!!*

Ft Lauderdale Fl   **3 Days**   **954-462-6000**
Bubier Park Downtown

All of the above "green craziness occurs again in West Palm Beach At Currie Park (On I.C.W.) In MARCH (Weekend Before St Patrick's Day) 3 Day Gala Is IRISH FEST ON FLAGLER 561-833-3711

'HOLIDAY' MAIN STREET
Since 1980
DEC - 2ND SUN   ATTEND 35,000

In a "cutey-pie" town few folks know exist!!! Safety Harbor's Main St leads to old renovated spring spa & town merchant area near pretty Safety Harbor.

> *By Invitation Only Vendors---300 Exhibitors Of Quality & Diversity---Food Court---Great Christmas Gifts*

Safety Harbor Fl   **1 Day**   **813-725-1562 Or 813-724-1555**
Near Tampa

FLORIDA STATE FAIR
Since 1898
FEB - 2ND & 3RD WEEK   ATTEND 475,000
Not attended a "state fair"? DON'T WAIT . . . . 325 A-C-R-E-S "be-bop" with events. Part of land is permanent home to CRACKER COUNTRY, historic Florida settlement with many town structures (even an operating "post office"). Midway "motion" (85 RIDES) spins, twirls, gyrates and roars. Even bungee jump, (yikes)!!

Headliners Of International Fame---Livestock Barns---Food, Baking, Sewing, Woodturning Competitions---GATLINBURG CRAFTSMEN'S FAIR, Royal Hanneford Circus, 5 Star Rodeo, Tiger, Bear Acts---Equestrian Center---Full Of Thrills, (Carriage Driving Competitions)---Clydesdale, Belgium, Percheron Pull Tandem Hitch, Log Skidding. Events Include Andalusians, Paso, Fino, Pony, Miniature Horses, Mounted Drill Teams, Tennessee Walkers & Arabians. Over 2,000 Horses Participate In 12 Days. Is There Food??? You've Got To Be Kidding!!!

Tampa, Fl   12 Days   800-345-3247   813-621-7821
Florida State Fairgrounds I-4 & U.S. 301

SCOTTISH HIGHLAND GAMES HERITAGE FESTIVAL
Since 1993
JAN - LAST SAT OR FEB - 1ST SAT   ATTEND 8,000
Bet ya' didn't know that 50 robust SCOTSMEN settled in Sarasota in 1885. That's the year "Jack Frost" sent a rare snowfall to the tropics. In spite, clans thrived & still call Sarasota home.

Heavy Athletic Games---Metal Weight Throws, 56 # Weight Toss, Caber Throw (19 Ft), Sheep Herding, Bag Pipe Bands From Scotland & Drumming---Big Tent Entertainment---Highland Dancing---Costumes, Food---Kiltie Band!!!

Sarasota, FL   1 Day   941-955-8187
Sarasota County Fairgrounds, Fruitville Rd

FESTIVAL MONTHLY REFERENCE

JANUARY
	PAGE
BOCA FEST	8
DOWNTOWN DELRAY FESTIVAL OF ARTS	9
LAS OLAS ART FAIR	9
KEY BISCAYNE ART FESTIVAL	11
ON THE GREEN	11
TASTE OF THE GROVE	17
SUPER BOWL CHILI COOKOFF	18
DADE MASSACRE RE-ENACTMENT	26
INTERNATIONAL PAVILION ON-THE-WATERWAY	52
INTERNATIONAL ART & ANTIQUE FAIR	52
FELLSMERE FROGLEG FESTIVAL	54
ART DECO WEEKEND	59

FEBRUARY
	PAGE
DOWNTOWN SARASOTA FEST-OF-THE-ARTS	7
COCONUT GROVE ART FEST	10
COCONUT GROVE BANYAN ARTS FEST	11
CHILI COOKOFF	18
HATSUME FAIR	20
EDISON FESTIVAL OF LIGHT	23
ILLUMINATED NIGHT PARADE	24
MEDIEVAL FAIR	27
RENAISSANCE FESTIVAL	27
FLORIDA RENAISSANCE FESTIVAL	31
SEMINOLE ARTS & CRAFTS	36
SWAMP CABBAGE FESTIVAL	36
SEMINOLE TRIBAL FAIR POW-WOW & PROFESSIONAL RODEO	36
INTERNATIONAL CARILLON FESTIVAL	38
WEST FAIR-BIGGEST RODEO IN THE EAST	41
SEAFOOD FEST	42
GRANT SEAFOOD FESTIVAL	43
EVERGLADES SEAFOOD FESTIVAL	43

	PAGE
GASPARILLA PIRATE FEST	48
INTERNATIONAL FOOD & WINE FAIR	52
MARDI GRAS LAKE WALES	55
QUILT & ANTIQUE SHOW	59
IRISH FEST	61
FLORIDA STATE FAIR	62
SCOTTISH HIGHLAND GAMES	62

MARCH
	PAGE
UNDER THE OAKS	7
MEET ME DOWNTOWN	7
ART FEST BY-THE-SEA	8
NAPLES DOWNTOWN FESTIVAL OF THE ARTS	10
12 HOURS OF SEBRING	12
ORANGE CUP REGATTA	16
PALM BEACH BOAT SHOW	16
STRAWBERRY FESTIVAL	19
FESTIVAL OF STATES	23
CIVIL WAR BATTLE RE-ENACTMENT	28
ITALIAN RENAISSANCE FESTIVAL AT VIZCAYA	29
RENAISSANCE FESTIVAL	30
BUCKINGHAM HISTORIC DAYS RE-ENACTMENT	31
SARASOTA JAZZ FEST	37
BLUEGRASS FESTIVAL	37
BLUEGRASS KISSIMMEE	37
FLORIDA STATE CHAMPIONSHIP BLUEGRASS FESTIVAL	35
ARCADIA RODEO	40
FLORIDA CRACKER TRAIL RIDE	41
BOYNTON BEACH G.A.L.A.	44
SANIBEL SHELL FAIR	46
ART & DESIGN FAIR	52
PIONEER PARK DAYS	58
IRISH FEST ON FLAGLER	61
FESTIVAL OF STATES	23

FESTIVAL MONTHLY REFERENCE

APRIL — PAGE
FLORIDA INTERNATIONAL AIR SHOW 4
SUN'N FUN E.E.A. FLY-IN 4
Z-HILLS EASTER BOOGIE 5
SIESTA FIESTA 10
ITALIAN FEST 17
BLOOMIN' ARTS FESTIVAL 20
FLORIDA HERITAGE FESTIVAL 30
FLORIDA WINE FEST 47
SAILOR CIRCUS 57

MAY
MAYFAIRE-BY-THE-LAKE 8
SHELL AIR & SEA SHOW 6
ARCADIA WATERMELON FESTIVAL 19
SUNFEST 53

JUNE
GOOMBAY 50
SUNSETS AT PIER 60 50

JULY
SUNCOAST OFFSHORE GRAND PRIX 14
VICTORIAN GARDEN PARTY-WORLD'S
LARGEST TOPIARY FESTIVAL 22
HEMINGWAY DAYS 25
ARCADIA RODEO 40

AUGUST
JAPANESE BON FESTIVAL 23
SHARKS TOOTH & SEAFOOD FEST 44
FOOD & WINE
APPRECIATION WEEKEND 47

SEPTEMBER
LAS OLAS ART FAIR 9
PIONEER FLORIDA DAY 28
POKER RUN 51

OCTOBER
OLD HYDE PARK VILLAGE ART FEST 9
FT LAUDERDALE INTERNATIONAL
BOAT SHOW 13
OKTOBER FEST 18

PAGE
JOHN'S PASS SEAFOOD FESTIVAL 42
SANDSCULPTING FESTIVAL 46
PUMPKIN FESTIVAL 53
RATTLESNAKE FESTIVAL 58
FANTASY FEST 60

NOVEMBER
FT MYERS BOAT SHOW 13
FLAPJACK FESTIVAL 17
GARDEN FESTIVAL 20
MUM FESTIVAL 22
POINSETTIA FESTIVAL 22
HOLIDAY FANTASY OF LIGHTS 24
ISLAND JUBILEE 25
HERITAGE FESTIVAL 26
HOLLYWOOD JAZZ 38
RIVERWALK BLUES 38
FALL FEST 39
ORANGE BLOSSOM STATE CHAMPIONSHIP
PROFESSIONAL RODEO 40
RUSKIN SEAFOOD & ARTS 42
LIGHTHOUSE GALLERY
FINE ART FESTIVAL 46
INTERNATIONAL FILM FESTIVAL 47
RIVER DAYZ & SEAFOOD SAMPLER 48
C.C.C. FESTIVAL 51
MELBOURNE HARBOR FESTIVAL 58

DECEMBER
WINTERFEST AIR SHOW 4
BRANDON BALLOON CLASSIC 5
AMERICA'S MOST WATCHED
BOAT PARADE 14
CORTEZ SEAFOOD FEST 19
RAMBLE-A-GARDEN-FESTIVAL 21
CHRISTMAS AT PINEWOOD
"A CITRUS CELEBRATION" 21
ANNA MARIA ISLAND WINEFEST 25
MICCOSUKEE INDIAN ARTS FESTIVAL 34
HOLIDAY MAIN STREET 61